to make a poem

Longman English and Humanities Series
Series Editor: Lee A. Jacobus,
University of Connecticut, Storrs

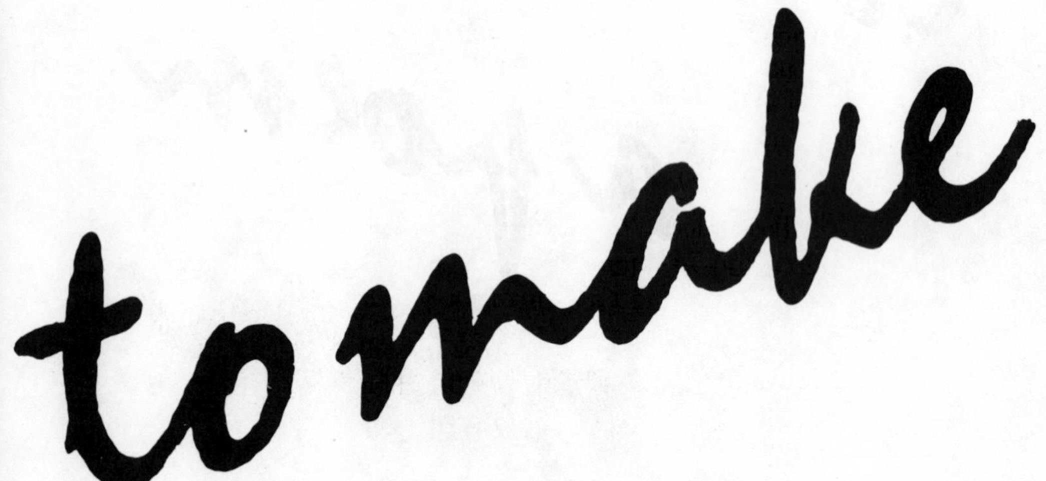

a poem

Alberta Turner

Longman
New York & London

To Make a Poem

Longman Inc., 1560 Broadway, New York, N.Y. 10036
Associated companies, branches, and representatives
throughout the world.

Developmental Editor: Gordon T. R. Anderson
Editorial and Design Supervisor: Joan Matthews
Interior Design: Diana Hrisinko
Manufacturing and Production Supervisor: Anne Musso

Library of Congress Cataloging in Publication Data

Turner, Alberta T.

(Longman English and humanities series)

1. Poetics. I. Title. II. Series.
PN1042.T83 1982 808.1 81-8442
ISBN 0-582-28236-5 AACR2

Manufactured in the United States of America

9 8 7 6 5 4 3

contents

preface

When I say that making poetry can be taught, hackles rise. When I say it can be taught by anyone to anyone, I hear growls. But wait. A poem comes from the same human need as a prayer, a curse, a lullaby, and a keen. A baby rocking and crooning nonsense syllables is making a "Song of Myself." The small boy on the playground taunts the larger one with epithets and boasts Homer could have used. To say that poetry is a universal form of expression is to say nothing more than that music and painting and dance are universal forms of expression. And to say that anyone can teach it is to say only that anyone can learn to examine and show others how to examine its emotional sources and the nature of its medium — language. Both student and teacher ask: How can emotion use language to satisfy its most urgent need, and how can it share and prolong that satisfaction by putting it into poems that will satisfy the same need in others? The answer can be learned and the skill taught.

To say the making of poems is natural and universal is not to say it is simple or easy, any more than it is simple or easy to guide a child from whistling a hopscotch tune to composing a concerto. But it is possible to train ears and fingers and learn musical notation. And it is possible to learn and teach the sound and rhythm of language, and the emotional power of image and metaphor and syntax. I believe it is also possible to learn and teach how to invite and recognize the first verbal grumblings of feeling, that is, to invite the subconscious mind by free association to present verbal raw material that the conscious mind can then learn to fashion into poems. These two steps, *inviting* and *making*, are dealt with in Parts

One and Two of this book. Part Three contains practical suggestions for inviting and making poems outside class and after the course is over.

I have taught — or tried to teach — using textbooks that are so tightly organized and furnished with such elaborate machinery that only their authors could use them efficiently. I have pored over teachers' manuals and been chagrined because I could not see how an author reached a specific interpretation. This book has no teacher's manual, and I do not expect those who use it to agree with all my interpretations. I have analyzed several poems to illustrate each principle, but have left it to the teachers and their students to apply those principles to the poems in the exercises, the poems that result from the exercises, and the Poems for Further Discussion. They may decide that a poem I thought handled a principle well did a poor job or vice versa. The important thing is that they use the principle to analyze the poem and decide for themselves whether it has succeeded or failed. Poetic tastes can't be legislated; they have to creep by underground runners.

Although a poem never illustrates only one poetic principle at a time, this book has focused on each separately. Since I hope the book will be used by beginning poets, I have sequenced the principles from simpler to more complex. Chapters on concrete imagery, followed by structure, rhythm, and sound precede those on multiple meanings and metaphor. Examples and exercises range from the level of analyzing nursery rhymes and making absurd sandwiches to analyzing villanelles and writing in complex metrical forms.

Since courses in writing poetry range from two-week enrichment programs to full-semester college workshops, I have arranged the book so that the course can be shortened or lengthened. Teachers in Poetry-in-the-Schools programs could teach the shortest and most elementary course by establishing the free-associative method (Part One, Chapter 1) in one day and spending a day each on the bare bones of imagery, structure, rhythm, sound, multiple meaning, and metaphor (Part Two), using only one example and one exercise to establish the principles of each, and skipping Part Three and Poems for Further Discussion entirely. They could spend every other day on establishing these principles and the alternate days on discussing with students the poems written from the exercises. They could use the book most fully in introductory poetry writing courses for college students by spending a week on each of the eight chapters in Parts One and Two and their resulting student poems — and the remaining time on workshops for editing student work written independently of the exercises, on journal keeping, and on analyzing additional poetic voices in Poems for Further Discussion. The book could even be used in a class in reading poetry, especially in conjunction with a good anthology. Students understand any artist's skill better by having tried the medium themselves.

On whatever level and in whatever time they decide to teach it, teachers need to modify this book by their own experience and adapt it to their own classes. I hope the exercises will tempt them to make up parallel ones of their own. The analyses of the poems should provoke them to contradict mine or to introduce and analyze additional poems to illustrate the same principles. I hope they will be tempted to try the exercises themselves and submit their own poems to the criticism of their workshops. They may wish to introduce more critical terms than I have used or to define further some that I hoped students already knew. Or teachers may want to emphasize the inductive quality of the course by teaching the principles treated in a chapter *before* they assign the class to read it.

This book will work best for flexible, imaginative teachers of flexible, imaginative students. If they work it hard, it will work them hard. And both will become poets.

Alberta Turner

acknowledgments

"Occupational Hazards" reprinted from THE NAMES OF A HARE IN ENGLISH by David Young by permission of the University of Pittsburgh Press. © 1979 by David Young.

"A Box for Tom" by James Tate. Copyright © 1976 by James Tate. Reprinted from VIPER JAZZ by permission of Wesleyan University Press.

"Wedding-Ring" from Denise Levertov, LIFE IN THE FOREST. Copyright © 1975 by Denise Levertov. Reprinted by permission of New Directions Publishing Corp.

"The Jacob's Ladder" by Denise Levertov. Copyright © 1961 by Denise Levertov Goodman. Reprinted by permission of New Directions Publishing Corp.

"Nothing Answers" from BEFORE SLEEP by Philip Booth. Copyright © 1976, 1977, 1978, 1979, 1980 by Philip Booth. Reprinted by permission of Viking Penguin Inc.

"In the Suburbs" by Louis Simpson. Copyright © 1963 by Louis Simpson. Reprinted from AT THE END OF THE OPEN ROAD by permission of Wesleyan University Press.

"Divine Love" by Michael Benedikt. Originally appeared in *The Sixties*, #10, © 1968; and in the author's *The Body*, (Wesleyan University Press) © 1968. Revision © 1982 by Michael Benedikt. Printed by permission of Michael Benedikt.

"Burning the Small Dead" from Gary Snyder, THE BACK COUNTRY. Copyright © 1968 by Gary Snyder. Reprinted by permission of New Directions Publishing Corp.

"Anecdote of the Jar" by Wallace Stevens. Copyright 1923 and renewed 1951 by Wallace Stevens. Reprinted from THE COLLECTED POEMS OF WALLACE STEVENS, by Wallace Stevens, by permission of Alfred A. Knopf, Inc.

"Shell III: Oracle" from BEAST FORMS by Leonard Trawick. Copyright © 1971 by Leonard Trawick. All rights reserved. Reprinted by permission of the author.

"Buffalo Bill's." Reprinted from TULIPS & CHIMNEYS by E. E. Cummings by permission of Liveright Publishing Corporation. Copyright 1923, 1925, and renewed 1951, 1953 by E. E. Cummings. Copyright © 1973, 1976, by Nancy T. Andrews. Copyright © 1973, 1976 by George James Firmage.

"The Computer's First Christmas Card" from THE SECOND LIFE by Edwin Morgan. Copyright © 1968 by Edwin Morgan and Edinburgh University Press. Reprinted by permission of Edinburgh University Press.

"Song of the Taste" from Gary Snyder, REGARDING WAVE. Copyright © 1968 by Gary Snyder. "Song of the Taste" first appeared in *Poetry*. Reprinted by permission of New Directions Publishing Corp.

"Joy Sonnet in a Random Universe" from COMING CLOSE AND OTHER POEMS by Helen Chasin. Copyright © 1968 by Yale University. Reprinted by permission of Yale University Press.

"Thirteen Ways of Looking at a Blackbird" by Wallace Stevens. Copyright 1923 and renewed 1951 by Wallace Stevens. Reprinted from THE COLLECTED POEMS OF WALLACE STEVENS, by Wallace Stevens, by permission of Alfred A. Knopf, Inc.

"Ariel" from ARIEL by Sylvia Plath. Copyright © 1965 by Ted Hughes. Reprinted by permission of Harper & Row, Publishers, Inc., and Olwyn Hughes.

"Why I Am Not Making My Last Trip Now" by Philip Levine. First appeared in *Field* No. 17, Fall 1977. Copyright © 1977 by Field Magazine/Oberlin College. Reprinted by permission of *Field*.

"Night" from Peter Everwine, KEEPING THE NIGHT. Copyright © 1977 (New York: Atheneum, 1977). Reprinted with the permission of Atheneum Publishers.

"Meeting My Class Called 'Easy Writer'" by William Stafford. Originally appeared in *Field* No. 10, Spring 1974. Copyright © Spring 1974 by Field Magazine/Oberlin College. Reprinted by permission of the author and *Field*.

"The First Days" from TO A BLOSSOMING PEAR TREE by James Wright. Copyright © 1974, 1977 by James Wright. Reprinted by permission of Farrar, Straus and Giroux, Inc.

"Called" by Michael S. Harper. First appeared in *Field* No. 10, Spring 1974. Copyright © 1974 by Field Magazine/Oberlin College. Reprinted by permission of the author and *Field*.

"In The Forest" from THE INTUITIVE JOURNEY AND OTHER WORKS by Russel Edson. First appeared in *Field* No. 9, Fall 1973. Copyright © 1973 by Field Magazine/Oberlin College. Reprinted by permission of the author.

"Wish For A Young Wife" from THE COLLECTED POEMS OF THEODORE ROETHKE by Theodore Roethke. Copyright © 1963 by Beatrice Roethke as Administratix of the Estate of Theodore Roethke. Reprinted by permission of Doubleday & Company, Inc.

"At the Edge of Town" from THAT OTHER ALONE by William Stafford. Copyright © 1973 by William Stafford. Reprinted by permission of the author.

"Range-Finding" from THE POETRY OF ROBERT FROST edited by Edward Connery Lathem. Copyright 1916, © 1969 by Holt, Rinehart and Winston. Copyright 1936, 1944 by Robert Frost. Copyright © 1964 by Lesley Frost Ballantine. Reprinted by permission of Holt, Rinehart and Winston, Publishers.

"Root Cellar" from THE COLLECTED POEMS OF THEODORE ROETHKE by Theodore Roethke. Copyright 1943 by Modern Poetry Association, Inc. Reprinted by permission of Doubleday & Company, Inc.

"Bears" from THE DIAMOND CUTTERS by Adrienne Rich. Copyright © 1955 by Adrienne Rich. Reprinted by permission of the author.

"The Spoon" from DISMANTLING THE SILENCE by Charles Simic. Copyright © 1971 by Charles Simic and George Braziller, Inc. Reprinted by permission of George Braziller, Inc.

"Eight O'Clock" from THE COLLECTED POEMS OF A. E. HOUSMAN. Copyright 1922 by Holt, Rinehart and Winston. Copyright 1950 by Barclays Bank Ltd. Reprinted by permission of Holt, Rinehart and Winston, Publishers, and by The Society of Authors as the literary representative of the Estate of A. E. Housman, and Jonathan Cape Ltd., publishers of A. E. Housman's COLLECTED POEMS.

"History of Ideas" and "When I Shall Be Without Regret" from COLLECTED POEMS AND EPIGRAMS by J. V. Cunnningham. Copyright © 1971 by J. V. Cunningham. Reprinted with the permission of The Ohio University Press, Athens.

"The Beautiful Changes" from THE BEAUTIFUL CHANGES, copyright 1947, 1975 by Richard Wilbur. Reprinted by permission of Harcourt Brace Jovanovich, Inc.

"Bells for John Whiteside's Daughter" by John Crowe Ransom. Copyright 1924 by Alfred A. Knopf Inc. and renewed 1952 by John Crowe Ransom. Reprinted from SELECTED POEMS, Third Edition, Revised and Enlarged, by John Crowe Ransom, by permission of Alfred A. Knopf, Inc.

"The Persian Version" from COLLECTED POEMS of Robert Graves, published by Doubleday 1961. Copyright © 1958, 1961 by Robert Graves. Reprinted by permission of Robert Graves and A. P. Watt Ltd.

"Some Last Questions" from W. S. Merwin, *The Lice*. Copyright © 1967 by W. S. Merwin (New York: Atheneum, 1967). Reprinted with the permission of Atheneum Publishers.

"Design" from THE POETRY OF ROBERT FROST edited by Edward Connery Latham. Copyright 1916, © 1969 by Holt, Rinehart and Winston. Copyright 1936, 1944, by Robert Frost. Copyright © 1964 by Lesley Frost Ballantine. Reprinted by permission of Holt, Rinehart and Winston, Publishers.

"Love Song" by David Young, from BOXCARS (The Ecco Press, 1973). Copyright © 1973 by David Young. Used by permission of The Ecco Press.

"Shame" by Richard Wilbur. © 1961 by Richard Wilbur. Reprinted from his volume ADVICE TO A PROPHET AND OTHER POEMS by permission of Harcourt Brace Jovanovich, Inc.

"To Paint the Portrait of a Bird" by Jacques Prévert, translated by Michael Benedikt. Taken from *Paroles* (1949). *Paroles* copyright © 1949 by Editions Gallimard. Copyright © 1974 by Michael Benedikt. Printed by permission of Georges Borchardt, Inc., and Editions Gallimard.

"The First Planet After Her Death" by Richard Somer. First appeared in *Field* No. 47, Spring 1971. Copyright © 1971 by Oberlin College. Reprinted by permission of Oberlin College.

"Hello" and "Where Are You" by Benjamin Péret translated by Michael Benedikt in *The Poetry of Surrealism* edited by Michael Benedikt. Editions le Terrain Vague. Copyright © 1971, 1972 by Editions le Terrain Vague. Reprinted by permission of Georges Borchardt, Inc., and Editions le Terrain Vague.

"The Bull Moses" from SELECTED POEMS by Ted Hughes. Copyright © 1959 by Ted Hughes. Reprinted by permission of Harper & Row, Publishers, Inc.; also reprinted by permission of Faber and Faber Ltd. from LUPERCAL by Ted Hughes.

"The Yawn Of Yawns" by Vasko Popa translated by Charles Simic. First appeared in *Homage To The Lone Wolf: Selected Poems 1956–1975* translated by Charles Simic, *Field Translation Series* No 2. Copyright © 1979 by Oberlin College. Reprinted by permission of Oberlin College.

"Diving Into the Wreck" is reprinted from DIVING INTO THE WRECK, Poems 1971–1972, by Adrienne Rich, with the permission of W. W. Norton & Company, Inc. Copyright © 1973 by W. W. Norton & Company, Inc.

"The Hour of Feeling" from SEARCHING FOR THE OX (1976) by Louis Simpson. Copyright © 1975 by Louis Simpson. By permission of William Morrow & Company.

"The Eye" by Richard Wilbur. Copyright © 1975 by Richard Wilbur. Reprinted from his volume THE MIND-READER by permission of Harcourt Brace Jovanovich, Inc.

"Occupational Hazards" by David Young. Copyright © 1979 by David Young. Reprinted by permission of the author.

"The Unknown Citizen" and "Epitaph on a Tyrant". Copyright 1940 and renewed 1968 by W. H. Auden. Reprinted from W. H. AUDEN: COLLECTED POEMS, by W. H. Auden, edited by Edward Mendelson, by permission of Random House, Inc., and Faber and Faber Ltd.

"The Moralist of Bananas" by Michael Benedikt. Originally appeared in *Field*, #6, © 1972 and in *The Prose Poem: An International Anthology* (Dell/Laurel) © 1976. Revision © 1982 by Michael Benedikt. Printed by permission of Michael Benedikt.

"The Crossed Apple" from THE BLUE ESTUARIES by Louise Bogan. Copyright © 1930, 1968 by Louise Bogan. Reprinted by permission of Farrar, Straus and Giroux, Inc.

"Matter" from BEFORE SLEEP by Philip Booth. COPYRIGHT © 1976, 1978, 1979, 1980 by Philip Booth. Reprinted by permission of Viking Penguin Inc.

"Next to of course god america i" by E. E. Cummings. Reprinted from IS 5 poems by E. E. Cummings, by permission of Liveright Publishing Corporation. Copyright 1926 by Horace Liveright. Copyright renewed 1953 by E. E. Cummings.

"a" by E. E. Cummings. © 1958 by E. E. Cummings. Reprinted from his volume COMPLETE POEMS 1913–1962 by permission of Harcourt Brace Jovanovich, Inc.

"The Sky was . . . ." Reprinted from TULIPS & CHIMNEYS by E. E. Cummings by permission of Liveright Publishing Corporation. Copyright 1923, 1925, and renewed 1951, 1953, by E. E. Cummings. Copyright © 1973, 1976 by Nancy T. Andrews. Copyright © 1973, 1976 by George James Firmage.

"If everything happens that can't be done" by E. E. Cummings. Copyright 1944 by E. E. Cummings; copyright 1972 by Nancy T. Andrews. Reprinted from COMPLETE POEMS 1913–1962 by E. E. Cummings by permission of Harcourt Brace Jovanovich, Inc.

"Anyone lived in a pretty how town" by E. E. Cummings. Copyright 1940 by E. E. Cummings; copyright 1968 by Marion Morehouse Cummings. Reprinted from COMPLETE POEMS 1913–1962 by E. E. Cummings by permission of Harcourt Brace Jovanovich, Inc.

"Helen" from SELECTED POEMS of H.D. Copyright 1925, 1953, © 1957 by Norman Holmes Pearson. Reprinted by permission of New Directions.

"Sweeney Among the Nightingales" from COLLECTED POEMS 1909–1962 by T. S. Eliot, copyright, 1936, by Harcourt Brace Jovanovich, Inc.; copyright © 1963, 1964 by T. S. Eliot. Reprinted by permission of the publisher and Faber & Faber Ltd.

"Missing Dates" from COLLECTED POEMS OF WILLIAM EMPSON, copyright 1949, 1977 by William Empson. Reprinted by permission of Harcourt Brace Jovanovich, Inc., and by William Empson and Chatto & Windus Ltd.

"Silent Poem," copyright © 1970 by Robert Francis, reprinted from ROBERT FRANCIS: COLLECTED POEMS 1936–1976, University of Massachusetts Press, 1976, copyright © by Robert Francis. Reprinted with the permission of The University of Massachusetts Press.

"Family in a Yard" and "The Store" from UP IN A BED by Stuart Friebert. Copyright © 1974 by Stuart Friebert. Reprinted by permission of the author.

"Full-Choked" from LIKE A DIAMOND BACK IN THE TRUNK OF A WITNESS'S BUICK by Jan Haagensen. Copyright © 1977 by Jan Haagensen. Reprinted by permission of the author.

"At Slim's River" by John Haines. Copyright © 1976 by John Haines. "At Slim's River," originally "At White River," first appeared in *Poetry Now*. Reprinted from *Cicada* by permission of Wesleyan University Press.

"Under the Apple Tree" and "Still Life" from CROSSING THE RIVER by Stratis Haviaras. Copyright © 1976 by Stratis Haviaras. Reprinted by permission of the author.

"Wood" from HOUSE OF WOOD, HOUSE OF SALT by Patricia Ikeda. Copyright © 1978 by Patricia Y. Ikeda. Reprinted by permission of the author.

"Counting the Mad" copyright © 1957 by Donald Justice. Reprinted from THE SUMMER ANNIVERSARIES by permission of Wesleyan University Press.

"Ars Poetica" and "Epitaph for a Postal Clerk" from NUDE DESCENDING A STAIRCASE by X. J. Kennedy. Copyright © 1956, 1958, 1959, 1960, 1961 by X. J. Kennedy. Reprinted by permission of Curtis Brown, Ltd.

"Variations on a Theme by William Carlos Williams" from THANK YOU AND OTHER POEMS by Kenneth Koch. Copyright © 1962 by Kenneth Koch. Reprinted by permission of the author.

"Poem for the Left and Right Hands" and "Sestina: Aqua and After" by Marilyn Krysl. Copyright © 1980 by Marilyn Krysl. Reprinted by the permission of the author.

"Song" from COLLECTED POEMS, 1954. Copyright © 1954 by C. Day Lewis. Reprinted by permission of Literistic, Ltd.

"Opuscules" from THE GLASSBLOWER'S BREATH by Thomas Lux. Copyright © 1976 by Thomas Lux. Reprinted by permission of the author.

"The Egg" from W. S. Merwin, *The Miner's Pale Children.* Copyright 1969, 1970 by W. S. Merwin (New York: Atheneum, 1970). Reprinted with the permission of Atheneum Publishers.

"The Extermination of the Shy" from THE NARROWS by Valery Nash. Copyright © 1980 by Valery Nash. Reprinted by permission of the author.

"Luggage" by Helga M. Novak, translated by Anne Maria Celona. First appeared in *Field* No. 9, Fall 1973. Copyright © 1973 by Field Magazine/Oberlin College. Reprinted by permission of *Field.*

"Dulce et Decorum Est" from COLLECTED POEMS of Wilfred Owen. Copyright © Chatto & Windus, Ltd., 1946, 1963. Reprinted by permission of New Directions Publishing Corp. "Dulce et Decorum Est" from THE COLLECTED POEMS OF WILFRED OWEN: Edited by C. Day Lewis. Reprinted by permission of The Owen Estate and Chatto & Windus Ltd.

"No, That Can't Be" by Erica Pedretti, translated by Stuart Friebert. Copyright © 1972 by Field Magazine/Oberlin College. First appeared in *Field* No. 7, Fall 1972. Reprinted by permission of *Field.*

"The Waking" from THE COLLECTED POEMS OF THEODORE ROETHKE by Theodore Roethke. Copyright 1953 by Theodore Roethke. Reprinted by permission of Doubleday & Company, Inc.

"Hush" from HUSH by David St. John. Copyright © 1975, 1976 by David St. John. Reprinted by permission of Houghton Mifflin Company.

"The Green Shepherd" by Louis Simpson. Copyright © 1963 by Louis Simpson. Reprinted from AT THE END OF THE OPEN ROAD by permission of Wesleyan University Press.

"Hunting, 13" from Gary Snyder, MYTHS & TEXTS. Copyright © 1960, 1978 by Gary Snyder. Reprinted by permission of New Directions Publishing Corp.

"In the Deep Channel" from STORIES THAT COULD BE TRUE by William Stafford. Copyright © 1960 by William Stafford. Reprinted by permission of Harper & Row, Publishers, Inc.

"How It Began" by William Stafford. Copyright © 1979 by Tom O'Grady. Reprinted by permission of *Hampden-Sidney Poetry Review* and by Tom O'Grady.

"Of Mere Being" by Wallace Stevens. Copyright © 1957 by Elsie Stevens and Holly Stevens. Reprinted from OPUS POSTHUMOUS, by Wallace Stevens, edited by Samuel French Morse, by permission of Alfred A. Knopf, Inc.

"Eating Poetry" from Mark Strand, *Reasons for Moving*. Copyright © 1968 by Mark Strand (New York: Atheneum, 1968). Reprinted with the permission of Atheneum Publishers.

"Do not go gentle into that good night" from THE POEMS of Dylan Thomas. Copyright 1952 by Dylan Thomas. Reprinted by permission of New Directions Publishing Corp. and David Higham Associates Limited.

"Locked Up in Tech High" by Leonard Trawick. First appeared in *Chicago Review* Vol. 26, No. 4, Copyright 1975 by the Chicago Review. Reprinted by permission of Chicago Review.

"Body Of —" and "Eight" from LID AND SPOON. Reprinted from LID AND SPOON by Alberta Turner by permission of the University of Pittsburgh Press. © 1977 by Alberta Turner.

"How Things Happen" and "On the Language Which Writes the Lecturer" from NAILING UP THE HOME SWEET HOME by Jeanne Walker. Copyright © 1980 by Jeanne Murray Walker. Reprinted by permission of the author.

"Love Calls Us to the Things of This World" from THINGS OF THIS WORLD, © 1956 by Richard Wilbur. Reprinted by permission of Harcourt Brace Jovanovich, Inc.

"This is Just to Say" from COLLECTED EARLIER POEMS of William Carlos Williams. Copyright 1938 by New Directions Publishing Corporation.

"The Five Dreams" by John Woods. First appeared in *Field* No. 12, Spring 1975. Copyright © 1975 by Field Magazine. Reprinted by permission of *Field*.

"Saint Judas" copyright © 1971 by James Wright. Reprinted from COLLECTED POEMS by permission of Wesleyan University Press. This poem first appeared in the *London Magazine*.

"The Second Coming" by W. B. Yeats. Copyright 1924 by Macmillan Publishing Co., Inc., renewed 1952 by Bertha Georgie Yeats. Reprinted by permission of Macmillan Publishing Co., Inc., and by M. B. Yeats, Anne Yeats, Macmillian London Limited; and A. P. Watt Ltd.

"When Helen Lived" from COLLECTED POEMS of William Butler Yeats. Copyright 1916 by Macmillan Publishing Co., Inc., renewed 1944 by Bertha George Yeats. Reprinted by permission of Macmillan Publishing Co., Inc., and by M. B. Yeats, Anne Yeats, Macmillan London Limited, and A. P. Watt Ltd.

"Leda and the Swan" from COLLECTED POEMS by William Butler Yeats. Copyright 1928 by Macmillan Publishing Co., Inc., renewed 1956 by Georgie Yeats. Reprinted by permission of Macmillan Publishing Co., Inc., and by M.B. Yeats, Anne Yeats, Macmillan London Limited, and A. P. Watt Ltd.

"The Poem Against the Horizon" by David Young. Copyright by David Young 1977. Reprinted by permission of the author.

to make a poem

part one

inviting the poem

If people ask, "How are you?" you tend to give different answers, depending on who asks and when and where. You say "Fine" to the boss, "Lousy" to a classmate who is going to take the same history test next hour, and to yourself, "I don't care whether I pass that test or not." In each case you know exactly what you mean. But you've made three contradictory statements about your feelings. You've said you're feeling fine, lousy, and defiant — all statements aimed at pleasing people who expect certain answers, people you want to satisfy. The boss expects to hear something that will translate as "OK, I'm ready for work"; your classmate expects to hear, "OK, I'm as worried as you are. That makes two of us"; your self wants to hear, "I'm tough and cool and unflappable." You are using language as we all do for practical purposes, to keep the rest of the world (including the critical part of ourselves) off our backs — that is, to cope.

But suppose you want to be honest, suppose you're curious to find out how you really feel and want to make someone else feel the same way? Just any conventional answer won't do if you are persuading a lover that you love him/her, expressing your fear of death, your pity for suffering, your hatred of cruelty, your need for a father, mother, God, or your bliss and well-being, your physical joy. The protective use of language has not prepared you to be so exact or so honest. Even if you answered "How are you?" with "I'm not sure yet; ask me later" or "Dim, unconscious" or even "Round, green, and slightly slippery," you would only imply that you wanted to shake off the question. The fact is that we often don't know our exact feelings. They have to be surprised out of us when we're not looking, as they are when someone suddenly steps on our foot or we drop a bag of groceries in the street or we're laid out on a psychiatrist's couch.

A poem is the verbal equivalent of such a surprise. When your poem succeeds, the people who read or hear it say, "Wow," "Yeah, that's how it is," "Ugh," "Ha!" When it fails, they say, "Oh, that again" or "So what!" When it succeeds, you yourself are surprised every time you read it; when it fails, you find it "blah" and throw it out.

To surprise yourself into discovering what you really mean is the first purpose of this book; to edit the words in which this surprise occurs into a poem that will surprise others is the second purpose. The first is an unconscious process and can only be induced. It provides the raw material of poems.

Imagine a box, any kind or size of box. On one page or in five minutes, whichever comes first, list all the things that might possibly come out of that box. Keep seeing it in your mind's eye and keep pulling things

1 reaching into the box

out at random, not expecting or looking *for* anything, but just grabbing and pulling, grabbing and pulling.

The following two lists were pulled out of two imaginary boxes. The authors then put them on the board, and the class examined them to see if they could detect what felt ideas had unconsciously surfaced.

1. T's LIST

My box is closed.

I open it, and out comes an awful smell.
I hold my nose with one hand and reach in with the other. Out come

orange peels	letter from home
egg shells	empty matchbook
soft onion	chicken leg
fish head	nicked wine glass
greasy paper	silk tie
chewed pencil stub	picture frame
my ring	plastic rose
squeezed tube	small yellow bird

The following questions guided the discussion of T's list. Various members of the class offered the answers:

Q. What do the items on this list have in common?
A. They all stink. They're all trash. They're no longer good for their original purposes.

Q. Have they all been the same kinds of things?
A. Some were food; some were luxuries, such as the silk tie and the wine glass; one, the plastic rose, was a fake decoration.
A. Some have practical uses, like the squeezed tube, the matchbook, and the chewed pencil.
A. Some suggest human relationships, such as the picture frame, the ring, the letter from home, and perhaps the yellow bird.

Q. Do the ring, the frame, the letter, and the bird suggest any particular relationship?
A. They might all belong to a broken engagement or marriage.

Q. Is there a perceivable sequence in the list?
A. From food at the beginning to personal relations at the end.

Q. Would any of the following come near to being a good title? "Loss," "I Hate Her," "A Common End"?
A. "Loss" suggests a similar regret for all the things on the list. Some of these seem to be more loathed than regretted.
A. "A Common End" is certainly true, since every person and thing must eventually be used up, worn out, or decayed.
A. But such a general and unemotional statement leaves out the anger, grief, disgust, and perhaps even the guilt implied by the broken relationship.
A. "I Hate Her" says that hate is the only feeling, yet since one doesn't hate mere garbage, it implies anger, regret, and disgust, perhaps even self-disgust. By telling less this title says more.

Q. If T. decides that anger, regret, and disgust join to form the dominating mood, what changes would you advise him to make in order to emphasize it? Would you remove anything?
A. The matchbook, squeezed tube, and pencil stub. They're neither irritating nor disgusting.

Q. Is the ring ambiguous? Do we need to know what kind of ring it is?
A. Probably not. In a list that has also a thrown-out letter from home and a discarded picture frame, we'd know the ring was a wedding or engagement ring. Don't insult the reader.

Q. In the present sequence the disgusting things tend to come first; the personal ones, which might be expected to suggest nostalgia or guilt, come at the end. Do you want to make these seem equally disgusting?

A. You could put a soft peach after the silk tie and another fish head after the picture frame. I thought the bird was disgusting. It's dead like the fish. Or is it an artificial bird?

When asked, T. didn't know. A lively discussion followed: some preferred the bird to be fake, like the plastic rose and the failed relationship; others insisted that the bird should be dead, and thus evidence of a relationship that had once been at least partly real. T. liked the animated response and decided to leave the yellow bird ambiguous.

T's list now read

I Hate Her

orange peels
egg shells
soft onion
fish head
greasy paper
my ring
letter from home
chicken leg
nicked wine glass
silk tie
soft peach
picture frame
fish head
plastic rose
small yellow bird

The disgust at real physical rottenness now includes such normally romantic objects as ring, wine glass, silk tie, rose, and yellow bird. The list now indicates to anyone who reads it that the whole relationship is rotten and deserves to be thrown out.

2. M's LIST

gold slippers, very pointy toes
six Christmas-tree ornaments, also gold
Mother's gold hatpin in gold paper
Grandfather's watch chain
gold bathtub faucet
gold lizard with green glass eyes
three oranges
milkweed stem coated with ice
ear of mildewed corn
gray pumpkin with a puckered chin
Jim before his hair was cut
Merthe's department store after they moved and left the windows empty
Mr. Watson's teeth

Q. Do you notice any repetitions in M's list?

A. The word *gold* is mentioned six times in the first half of the list. Its presence is implied in watch chain, oranges, and Mr. Watson's teeth. Its former presence is implied in pumpkin, corn, and in Jim before his hair was cut.

Q. Does gold mean the same thing each time?

A. No. Sometimes it means actual metal ornaments: hatpins, watch chains, ornamental faucets, brooches. Sometimes it means things colored to look like gold: slippers, Christmas-tree ornaments.

A. Sometimes it means health, things in a natural, undamaged state: oranges, pumpkin before it rotted, corn before mildew discolored it, head before its golden hair was cut.

Q. What does it mean in Mr. Watson's teeth?

A. Gold fillings are an attempt to preserve a natural thing, a tooth, which in the long run can't be preserved.

Q. Does the list sequence these things at random or progress from all of one kind to all of another?

A. Most of the artificial things are in the first half; most of the decayed natural things come toward the end.

Q. Do you see any need for Mr. Watson's teeth to come last?

A. They are the only things that combine decay and the attempt to stop it with metal.

Q. Given the unconscious emphasis on the different meanings of gold in this list, M. seems to be saying something about kinds of permanence. Is she saying that gold lasts, but natural things do not?

A. Physically it lasts.

Q. What do you mean *physically*? Is there something about gold that doesn't last?

A. The gold hatpin, lizard brooch, faucet, and pointy-toed slippers go out of style. The function of the gold fillings for teeth is destroyed when the person with filled teeth dies.

Q. Would any of the following titles include both these meanings? "Good as Gold," "All That Glitters," "The Gold We Have and the Gold We Lose," "Gold"?

A. "Good as Gold" suggests virtue. No one is acting virtuous or otherwise on this list.

A. "All That Glitters" is part of a proverb, "All that glitters is not gold." Gold as true and glitter as false doesn't seem to be the central contrast here.

A. "The Gold We Have and the Gold We Lose" doesn't say that in one way or another we lose them both.

A. "Gold" would probably be best, because that title allows all the meanings the reader can find. It starts one looking at the usual, familiar kinds, such as ornaments, and moves one to less expected golds, such as those that ought to be there but have been lost. Without that title the reader might forget that they were once gold too.

Q. Is there anything on the list you would leave out because it doesn't point to gold as either natural or artificial treasure?

A. Milkweed, Merthe's department store.

Q. Is there anything that seems merely to repeat?

A. Grandfather's watch chain is like Grandmother's gold hatpin.

Q. If you don't need both, which would you remove?

A. The watch chain; it's so often used in stories and ads about the "old times" that it sounds secondhand.

Q. Does it matter what kind of Christmas-tree ornaments are meant? Would balls, bells, birds, or gilded fruit tell you more?

A. Bells would suggest religion; fruit would contrast nicely with the decayed corn and pumpkin.

A. Balls are commonest and most traditional.

A. Birds would remind us of Fabergé or Yeats' golden bird of Byzantium. (After the class discussed and could not agree, M. chose bells, because she said religion is also an attempt to preserve and continue men's lives.)

Q. The list now contains ten things, the first five artificial, the next four natural, and the last a combination of the two, as if M. were saying, "Not this nor this, but this." How could she set it on the page to represent these divisions of idea?

A. ___________ ___________
___________ ___________
___________ ___________
___________ ___________
____
____

A. Or

____
____
____
____
____

____
____
____
____

____

Q. Now that the two groups are set apart, do you notice that one item doesn't match the rest of its group? Which one?

A. Oranges. They are a natural gold, but unlike the other members of their group, they haven't lost their goldness.

A. You might say *soft* oranges or *shrunken* oranges or *gray* oranges.

Q. Since the two ideas are of about the same importance and the two groups about the same length, could you make them both the same number of lines to emphasize the contrast?

A. You could take out one of the first group. The gold faucet is not quite the same kind of gold as the others in that group. It's something only the very rich and decadent would own, not everyone's kind of ornament, like a hatpin or Christmas-tree decorations.

A. Or you could add one to the second group. How about *fallen leaves*? (Several members of the class protested that *fallen leaves* was too familiar, but liked the idea of balance.)

Q. How about adding Mr. Watson's teeth to the second group?

A. Since Mr. Watson's teeth share the meaning of both groups, they should stand alone. (M. agreed and removed the gold bathtub faucet.)

M's final list read

GOLD

Gold slippers, very pointy toes
six Christmas-tree bells, also gold
Grandmother's gold hatpin in
gold paper
gold lizard with green glass eyes
three soft oranges
ear of mildewed corn
gray pumpkin with a puckered
chin
Jim before his hair was cut
Mr. Watson's teeth

Now take the lists you have drawn from your own imaginary boxes and ask

1. Which things on my list seem to go together? In what way? Subject? Attitude? Other?
2. Is there movement in the sequence from one *thing* to another, one *action* to another, one *attitude* to another?
3. Is there any title that might point to what that list seems to be saying?

When you decide which title fits, ask the following:

1. Do any items on my list repeat each other? Could any be removed without changing the meaning?
2. Are there any items I should add to the list to complete the felt idea?
3. Are all the items remaining on my list in the same sequence as the movement of my idea? If not, could I rearrange them? Group them? Repeat some of them in other positions?

Neither your "final" lists nor T's and M's are finished poems, but they do illustrate the psychological process by which all poems start: all your experiences are stored in your subconscious mind under the lock and key of your feelings about them — the dog that bit you, the banana peel you slipped on, the way the culvert smelled when you crawled through it, the soft thing you stepped on in the dark on the stairs. When you have recalled them, you can name them *scary, painful, disgusting*. But unrecalled, they make you feel pained or disgusted or scared without knowing why. You may want to convey your unease, but you don't understand it. To do this you must put yourself through the experience itself again. You can't *make* this happen, but you can *let* it happen. You can't find something by trying if you don't know what you're looking for, but if you forget it and let go, it may come to you.

Suppose, for example, you want a Christmas present for your father. He "has everything." Though you've known him all your life, you can't think of a specific thing he would like. But walking through the toy department you notice a table of those round glass balls with snowmen in them that you shake to make it snow. And in your mind you see him passing your desk, where you're doing your math homework, and turning over your snowman paperweight that he gave you when you were six. At that moment you know you have the right gift. Similarly, the poem idea that you really want to find can't be ordered, but can always be invited by emptying your mind and letting random bits of experience flow into the vacuum. This process of emptying the mind and letting bits of experience flow into it at random is called *free association.*

Many of the best-known poets writing today have said that they use some form of free association to invite the first drafts of their poems:[1]

> *William Stafford*: "My poem started from amid random writing I was doing in my usual morning attempts to scare up something by putting anything down that came to mind."
>
> *David Young*: "My process of writing is to begin with free association, then decide gradually on a theme and structure."
>
> *Dennis Schmitz*: "Most of my poems begin in free-association . . . I discover the subject as the poem develops."
>
> *Donald Justice*: "I was typing out tetrameter couplets about nothing in particular . . . trying to warm up, not feeling altogether responsible for what my fingers might find to say."
>
> *Peter Klappert*: "I do not start with an *idea*, a *theme*, or an *abstraction*: one finds out what he is doing in the process of doing it."

Even poets who start a poem with a conscious felt idea free associate, on purpose or instinctively, to explore that idea in directions they have not foreseen.[2]

> *Robert Wallace*: "For a week or so the idea kept turning up and I tried to get a verbal start, but nothing happened until the phrase 'no one but him' popped into my head."

[1] The following quotations are from *50 Contemporary Poets*, ed. A. Turner (New York: Longman, 1977), pp. 151, 169, 269, 292, 357.
[2] *Ibid.*, pp. 190, 324.

Maxine Kumin: "It was to be a poem of lambs. . . . I couldn't do it. It didn't work. . . . I don't remember how long after, but certainly several weeks, I picked up the worksheets again and began fiddling — you might call it free-associating — and what came back to consciousness was the terrible memory of the slaughter of the wild horses in Idaho."

Whether they sit down at the same time each day (Stafford), listen to music (Jon Anderson), doodle on the typewriter (Justice), brood on a phrase (Wallace), or just free associate in a specific mood (Klappert), poets will invite a poem by emptying the mind of preconceptions and letting it drift.

With practice you too can develop the habit of emptying your mind to invite the raw material of poems. For example:

1. Suppose you have nothing particular to say and no particularly strong feeling at the moment, you could invite a poem by pushing an imaginary shopping cart through a supermarket or a toy store; closing your eyes and imagining you put a spoonful of something strange into your mouth; imagining a knock at the door and saying, "Come in." Any one of these will recall something your subconscious mind has been saving and will present it in unexpected combinations. It might present something you thought you liked in a context that makes you realize you actually fear it, like the old lady next door who brought you cookies, bending over an oven, peering into a furnace, lifting the lid off a garbage can. Or it might present the uncle who always smiled at you, stripping an ear of corn with pointy teeth, cutting wood with a chain saw, grinding his clutch. Or it might present something you think you like in such clear detail that you like it even better.
2. Suppose someone you know well has died. You know how you feel, but how to make another person feel it? You know that "I'm lonely," "I miss you," "I remember all the good times" have been said hundreds of times in the same situation. You don't want the poem that expresses *your* feeling to sound as if it might have been written by anyone at all. Your experience is unique. Try letting go: write the person's name, then anything that name suggests — phrases that person used, gestures, jackets, socks, chairs he sat on, the annoying way he slammed the door — nothing necessarily associated with grief. When you have a couple of pages of these, or when the flow slackens, leave it. Come back, hours later, perhaps

next day, after your conscious mind has been entirely on something else. Then see which particulars best suggest the feeling of loss.

3. Suppose something makes you vaguely uncomfortable and you don't know why. Suppose somebody has asked you to forgive him. You've said you would, but you don't feel good about it. Perhaps there was nothing to forgive, perhaps you didn't mean it — nothing you can explain. Put the word *forgive* at the top of a page. Put down all the expressions you've ever heard the word used in and phrases you've read or used yourself. Write fast. When they stop coming easily and you think hard to find one, go do something else; come back later and repeat the process, without rereading what you wrote last time. Do this four or five times, then reread. Among the clichés and repetitions you will find the full range of what the word means to you, in phrases that demonstrate your contradictory feelings. Or take the same word, *forgive,* and look it up in the largest historical dictionary, the *Oxford English Dictionary.* Every meaning the word has ever had is there, embedded in quotations from the time when each shade of meaning came into the language. You will find pages of them. Now jot down phrases that attract you, as phrased in the dictionary or rephrased in your own words or in a mixture of the two. Leave. Come back later. Select what creates the principal emotion or combination of emotions the word has for you. Try doing the same for *creep, wear, right,* or *bliss.*
4. If you want to discover how you feel about a person, trim a Christmas tree for him or her or imagine yourself opening his closet or packing her a suitcase.
5. If you want to learn what kind of person you yourself are, empty your purse or pockets and arrange the contents in an order of increasing importance; walk through a paradise of your own choosing and describe what you see, who comes to meet you, what you are asked to do; list what you would do to get rid of the "blahs"; fill a wastebasket with things you would like to throw away; turn the pages of a Sears catalog fast and jot down what attracts your eye.

You will notice that your free-associated jottings are not always lists of single concrete words. The list is only one way to start a poem. It is an especially good way because single words, especially concrete words, are at their most suggestive and flexible. A sentence has already selected one of a word's meanings and closed out the surprises that might come from putting an uncommitted word next to one you have never seen it with before.

But lists of other units, such as questions, directions, phrases, dialog, even reflective comments that contain subordinate clauses, can also be free-associated and moved as wholes to make surprising combinations. And once you have selected and sequenced and decided what felt idea has surfaced, the separate items can be rephrased and joined in any syntax you choose. Unfocused free association, that which is not started by a box or a question, is likely to take several forms in the space of one ten-minute session. The important thing for beginning poets is to empty their minds and let *any* words in.

EXERCISES

1. Examine, in Poems for Further Reading, the list poems "Silent Poem," by Robert Francis, and "Hunting, 13" from *Myths and Tests*, by Gary Snyder. What felt ideas do the selection and sequencing of their lists reveal? How do you know?
2. Invite the raw material of a poem by any of the free associations suggested in Examples 1–5, on pages 10–11. Share it with the other members of your class. Ask them to help you identify your felt idea and to suggest additions, omissions, and sequencing that will reveal your idea more clearly.

As you have discovered by now, recognizing the pattern of feeling and idea, the germ of a poem, in your raw material is not automatic. Your two pages or ten minutes of free association will present the bits of experience as they appeared in the box exercise: a pile of unorganized, repetitious, incomplete, even contradictory fragments. You may see several possible ideas there. Which will you isolate, which drop, which allow to contradict each other, that is, which do you mean? You try this selection in that order, that selection in this order. If you don't come to a satisfying conclusion in one sitting, you may want to put the material aside, then free associate again in a day or a week, then select and sequence from the expanded material. The following drafts illustrate the process by which one felt idea went from free association on the word *paradise* to completed poem:

PARADISE (final draft)

No beak wears my hood
or nostril my ring
No mouth carries my apple to the oven

I can lie down in front of a plow
and no one will catch his breath
because he didn't see me in time

Draft I (initial free association)

Legs are good and plenty of them
shoes dyed green and frail
and flames for every grain
and age of wood

None of these are asked of me
I do not *have* to be cruel

My dog has brought me slippers or his leash
No hand will shake salt
because I carve a cutlet
I can lie under a plow and be cut
through and no one will catch breath
and wish he hadn't done it

2 freeing the felt idea

"Speak and you shall be listened to"
Not this bullfrog. I croak my own
translation. I climb clouds rung by
rung, without breaking them
sit in the crotch of grasses and swing my legs
No one will pay for what I do —
      pay me, pay for, pay you

Draft 2 (the first conscious selection, which begins to reveal the pattern that the poet found in the random material)

Iron shoes for tender hooves
{soles dyed green and frail
{leather stretched and dried frail
flames for every grain and age of wood.

None of these are mine.
I do not *have* to be {cruel.
                      {unkind

No dog { has brought me his leash.
{ brings
No hand will shake salt
because I crave a rib
I can lie down on the ground and the plow turn me under
and no one will catch his breath
and wish he hadn't done it.

"Speak and you must be listened to."
Not this bullfrog. I never was a prince
I shake out clouds without tearing them,
I do not pay for what I { do
{ am.

Between the first draft and the second the poet decided that "In my paradise I do not have to be cruel" was the poem's point and took out at least part of what seemed to say something else. The speaker's good legs were removed; the human shoes became stretched and dried. In the third stanza the slippers were removed; their suggestion of comfort and love did not support the idea of cruelty. In the fourth stanza the idea of freedom with power to do and be what one pleases suggested by "I croak my own translation" and "sit in the crotch of grasses and swing my legs" gave way to a refusal to choose. By the third draft the first stanza had become a forge for binding horses to servitude, and the last stanza had become entirely a rejection of power. The meaning of *cruelty* had been broadened to *power.*

Draft 3

Iron forge for iron shoes,
flame for every grain of wood,
hooves split and dried and split —
None of these are mine;
I don't have to be cruel.

No dog brings me a leash,
no knee shakes because I carve a rib.
I can lie down in front of a plow
and no one will catch his breath
because he didn't see me in time.

"Get? Make? Choose?
Not this frog. Never was a prince,
cannot sit on a plate, will not
dampen a bed. I cannot pay
for what I own.

Much later, on the principle that indirection is more forceful than direct explanation, the poet removed all but the second stanza and changed the first two examples in it to less familiar ones that made the same point. The felt idea that emerged in the fourth and final draft was, "In my paradise I do not have to exert power over animals by using them for work or food, nor over people by making them feel guilt."

David Young describes how he discovered the felt idea of a poem that first appeared as a cluster of sound, rhythm, and image:

OCCUPATIONAL HAZARDS[1]

Butcher

If I want to go to pieces
I can do that. When I try
to pull myself together
I get sausage.

Bakers

Can't be choosers. Rising
from a white bed, from dreams
of kings, bright cities, buttocks,
to see the moon by daylight.

Tailor

It's not the way the needle
drags the poor thread around.
It's sewing the monster together,
my misshapen son.

Gravediggers

To be the baker's dark opposite,
to dig the anti-cake, to stow
the sinking loaves in the unoven —
then to be dancing on the job!

[1] *50 Contemporary Poets, op. cit.*, pp. 350–352.

Woodcutter

Deep in my hands
as far as I can go
the fallen trees
keep ringing.

My process of writing is to begin with free association, then decide gradually on theme and structure. Often a cluster of sounds form around a rhythm that also constitutes an image. That was the case here: I began with the Woodcutter section, especially the first two lines, then, very shortly after, the other two. When I had this section, I didn't know what I wanted to do with it; it seemed too slender to be a poem on its own. Then, suddenly, a day or so later, the phrase "Bakers can't be choosers" popped into my head and I had the main subject and structure of the poem.

I think there were about twenty drafts, some of them differing very minutely from one another. Time intervals were as little as fifteen minutes, as much as a month (poem begun around Christmas and finished in June, which is longer than I usually take, but I was abroad and working more desultorily). The poem both shrank and expanded. There were seven sections at one time, seven occupations, and finally there were five. The structure did not change in essence once I had conceived the subject and knew I wanted a series of speakers, of occupations. And tone changed only in the sense that I needed to find a way to link the silliness of the pun with the gravity of the Woodcutter section, so that revision was a gradual bridging between those two tonal extremes (although I never put it that way to myself until just now). Which lines remained unchanged? The original woodcutter lines, the baker pun, the first two lines of the Tailor section, the last line of the gravedigger. Why? I guess I felt they worked the way I wanted them to. The changes fell more in the area of imagery and connotation. I was trying to bring all the elements of the poem up to the quality I felt was in the best lines, a certain kind of resonance inhering mainly in the imagery but supported by sound and movement, and of course "voice." A little like thickening and seasoning a sauce. Also there was some tightening of relationships, e.g., the gravediggers thinking of themselves as opposites to the bakers, a last-minute inspiration at something like the next-to-last draft.

The composition of "A Box for Tom," by James Tate, illustrates the same process of separating the felt idea from the random or given material. In this case Tate had less trouble identifying the idea that old clothes are history than in finding the right humorous-serious tone to show his respect for them.

A BOX FOR TOM[2]

These exquisite rags carry
the lice of history.
They've been there,
great cities turning in the night,
lamplit barges haunting
industrious rivers,
weepy adieus at a farm
alone on the edge of the prairie.

Here are worthy garments
to be worn as camouflage
for your lofty character,
to hide your misfit spirit;
fit for slumming in some
of the very best restaurants,
at home with snobs who snub you,
and generally causing a stir
among birds of flight and terrapins.

You can retrace an old ghost's
bad luck back to the pot of gold
in a pool hall getting a start,
then missing, falling, staining
everything to match his shoes
which were covered with doglime,
angel hair and bad news.

I had been sitting at my desk staring into a closet full of old clothes. I quite often go into trances before I write, and this meditation on some old clothes I hadn't seen for three years because of their inaccessibility in a trunk in somebody's basement was beginning to take me down lively but sad thoughts concerning the history of clothes, as if they had a life of their own — which I think they do.

It has been pointed out to me a number of times that I sometimes dress rather, shall we say, irregularly. I have always held on to clothes as long as I could possibly get by wearing them without being arrested. I wear shirts, slacks, shoes that I had fifteen years ago. If I like something it is alive for me. That's not strange: If you can let a plant depress you, why not love a sock? Well, such were my thoughts as I stared into my closet. And I was thinking about a friend of mine with whom I have an old, standing joke: I give him clothes no one else would wear on a bet, and Tom wears them with the same instinctive love of clothes that have been around as I do.

When I started the poem I wasn't sure where it would go. I didn't care, it felt good. So I wrote very roughly, finding myself making images; the poem obviously wanted to express itself in images. I was thinking about my friend Tom, and I was thinking of him in some of the old cast-offs I unloaded on him this past summer, really alarming duds. The poem had a strong rhythm and was rather melodious. I started to go wrong in the poem after nine lines in the first draft. I started to make a serious poem cute, which was cheapening what I really wanted to say on the subject.

[2] *50 Contemporary Poets, op. cit.*, pp. 318–321.

Draft I

GOOD WILL

here are some garments, to be worn as camouflage
for your lofty character, to hide your obese spirit
fit for slumming in some of your very best restaurants
at home with snobs who snub you, and generally causing
a stir among birds of flight and terrapins.

these exquisite rags carry the lice of history!
they've been there, great cities turning in the night,
lamplit barges haunting industrious rivers,
weepy adieus at a farm alone somewhere on the prairie.

~~if you don't like them fir d some naked bum~~
~~who will wear them, they've still got miles to go.~~

~~they never were the fashion, but they blended in~~
~~as bad taste will. the no count dude who accepts them~~
can retrace ~~my own~~ someone else's bad luck back to the pot of gold.
in a pool hall, ~~spilling barbecue, so much for white cords~~
getting a start somewhere, then falling, staining everything.

On the subject of subjects, I should interject here that I was conscious of having a subject. Many poems, what turn out to be poems, start for me with any kind of free association. I like to start out of the air and *then* find a subject, if at all, later. But recently I had felt the need to get back to the kind of poem that addresses some thing, some instance of dealing with a defined area.

But back to the poem. Four lines that were no good, that degraded the subject and I knew it; and finally three lines that got back to the mood of the first nine lines, though I knew there was a lot of work ahead to make anything of them. The first draft was just seeing what could come out; I did use twelve of the original sixteen lines but they had to be shaped and refined with some sharpening of the language — adjectives and various modifiers were weak. The word "some" got to be a problem; I like the word, as bland as it is; but I recognized that it was overused, not justified, and responsible for heightening the danger of a plague of melancholia indigenous to the subject.

Draft 2

GOOD WILL

These exquisite rags carry the lice of history!
They've been there, great cities turning in the night,
lamplit barges haunting industrious rivers,
weepy adieus at a farm alone somewhere on the prairie.
Here are some garments, to be worn as camouflage
for your lofty character, to hide your obese spirit,
fit for slumming in some of ~~your~~ the very best restaurants
at home with snobs who snub you, and generally causing
a stir among birds of flight and terrapins,
can retrace someone else's bad luck back to the pot of gold,
in a pool hall, getting a start somewhere, then falling, staining
    everything.

What I wrote down as a second draft didn't add much to the first draft: I just wanted to see how it read with the trash lines excised and the existing lines rearranged. I liked the possibilities of the pool hall at the end, but the ending as it stood now was fake, hokey, and I wanted something with a strong, clear statement, with some hint of pathos to it, hopefully not overdone. The poem seemed to veer too quickly back and forth from the rather gentle levity of a line like "and generally causing/a stir among birds of flight and terrapins" to, say, the ending. I liked the "terrapins" line and was going to try to hang on to it as long as I could, though I knew it was slightly too light for the rest of the poem.

Where the poem went from there is not really all that far, but the steps were essential and paid off in lifting it into life. I wanted to go back to some free association, some doodling, to see if I could get something further, hopefully an extension, an appropriate ending. I wrote down what I at first thought were three outrageous lines; I didn't like them and didn't take them seriously: "to match his shoes/which were covered with dogshit/angel hair and bad news." The syntax sounded too poetic, maybe gimicky.

I tried a third draft. The long lines of the first two drafts didn't seem to be working, though, in a way, I was happy I had started the poem that way; I think they influenced the sounds and rhythm. I cut the lines nearly in two, and wanted to try stanzas. At this point in the poem, I might add, I still considered many doors open; I was still willing for it to change its character entirely if it had a good excuse.

Draft 3

A Box for Tom

~~GOOD WILL~~

These exquisite rags carry
the lice of history.
They've been there,
great cities turning in the night,
lamplit barges haunting
industrious rivers,
weepy adieus at a farm
alone ~~somewhere on~~ on the edge of the prairie.

Here are some garments
to be worn as camouflage
for your lofty character,
to hide your ~~obese~~ misfit spirit;
fit for slumming in some
of the very best restaurants,
at home with snobs who snub you,
and generally causing a stir
among birds of flight and terrapins.

You can retrace ~~someone else's~~ an old ghost's
bad luck back to the pot of gold
in a pool hall getting a start.
~~somewhere~~, ~~then~~ then missing falling,
staining everything,
to match his shoes
which were covered with dog~~shit~~lime,
angel hair and bad news.

Changing "somewhere on the prairie" to "on the edge of the prairie" was a move in the right direction. I knew that terms had to be more defined. So, brandishing my razor, I changed "someone else's bad luck" to "an old ghost's bad luck." Also I dropped the "somewhere" in the penultimate line of the poem; it wasn't adding anything except more drippy melancholy. Then I reconsidered the lines I had written down after the second draft: I thought, why not give it a try, see what it feels like.

I added them to the fourth [and final] draft. To my surprise I liked them. They were slightly bold and dramatic, but now I felt with the changes that had been made the poem might be able to hold them. Yes, they were growing on me; I was beginning to like them a lot. Reading the poem to myself again, looking for weak spots, I realized that the phrase "obese spirit" in the fourth line of the second stanza wasn't very clear; it could mean a number of things and I wasn't certain I wanted all of them. "Misfit" seemed appropriate; I liked the sound and sound was playing a sizable role in the choices that had to be made within this poem. It added a firmness. The sound and the rhythm were in charge of convincing everybody that what I was saying was true. I gave a great deal of thought also to the word "dogshit." In this case I liked the sound; it went well with "start" three lines above; and I also liked the harshness of the word. But that is where I worried: Was it trying to sound too "tough"? I finally thought it was. "Doglime" was different altogether, but now I realized it was best; the poem needed to be softened there, toned down.

Throughout the poem is trying to go back and forth on this matter of sentiment. It has an easy way about it that should help facilitate, accommodate, the paradoxical and contradictory things the poem has to say. Conning the watchdog. It ends on a low note but hopefully love has embued the clothes; life has not been wasted on them.

EXERCISES

1. Each of the following student poems was generated from the following page of free association in a poet's journal. What felt idea do you think made the selection in each case? What makes you think so?

SAMPLE PAGE FROM A POET'S JOURNAL

Cows that fatten — piebald cows and
little Three-Mile-Islands full of cream.
Why am I angry? The sky is piebald too. It's hot.
The chickens are dying, and they won't breed.

The car seat is all upholstered in mouse pelts, and the cat is under
the driver's seat.
It's hot. Ice slides across the tray.
Blatz tastes like brick dust, ground brick.
What do I mean? Do I matter?
Those mice did. So many I'll have to raise my umbrella.
Scalding rain. Beaches of tiny faces,
lifted, their mouths open.
Why am I angry?
What name has the spray can painted on the sea wall?
The sand, blowing, has half-blasted it away.

STUDENT POEMS

a.

WILLARD ISLAND

The sky is piebald
It's hot
The chickens are dying, and they won't breed.
The car seat is upholstered in rat pelts
and the cat is under the driver's seat.
Ice slides across the tray.
Blatz tastes like brick dust.
Beaches of beady-eyed faces, lifted,
their mouths open.
What name has the spray can painted
on the sea wall?
The sand, blowing, has half-blasted
it away.

MARY LOUISE ADAMS

b.

FAT CAT

A cat is in the driver's seat
One tabby paw on the horn
Black cap pulled rakishly . . .
Over one cold grey eye.

The tiger-striped limo moves through the crowd.
    A sea of big pink ears
    Pairs of bright, expectant eyes
    And tiny open mouths
    All crying.
            For a glimpse,
                    A word.

From Fat Cat.

And Fat Cat
Lounges against rare mouse-pelt upholstery,
In long Persian fur
Diamond stickpin at his throat.
Fifth Avenue all the way.

MICHELLE DECKER

c. **"BALK"**

"O Herbert, not tonight."
                    "Balk."
"Because —"
                    "Balk, Balk."
"We're going to die."
                    "Balk. Balk."
"I tell you, the sky is falling."
                    "Balk."
"Our Three Mile Island will never be the same."
                    "Balk. Balk."
"Well, I've just told everybody."
                    "Balk."
"I told Elsie. That fat ol' cow
    told me I was full of it."
                    "Balk. Balk. Balk."
"Those mice romping in the rain,
    I told them to get under cover."
                    "Balk."
"With open mouths they laughed."
                    "Balk."

"Then I told that cute little Fox."
"Balk."
"The one that lives behind the oak tree."
"Balk. Balk."
"He's the only one who didn't look
at me in disbelief.
"He said he knew exactly what I was
talking about, but not to worry."
"Balk."
"Then he got ready to go to work."
"Balk, Balk."
"Oh you know, that nuclear power plant."
"Balk."

CAROL HEINZ

d.

Their mouths open
they breed
they fatten
they keep on breeding
It's hot — no produce
they repeat/repeat/repeat
So many
blasted sand
keep the breeding
and the not dying

TERRY WEBER

e.

Why am I angry?
It's hot — Blatz tastes like brick dust.
Why am I angry?
What name has the spray can painted on the sea wall?
Why am I angry?
Because some errant graffitist has
written on the seaside?
Or because the sand, blowing, has half-
blasted the name away?

JENNIFER BASTASIC

f.

Why am I angry?
It's hot, fool.
Why am I angry?
It's hot, fool, and the Blatz tastes like brick dust
and Three Mile Island covered everything
with brick dust.
Why am I angry?
It's hot, fool, and the Blatz tastes like brick dust
and Three Mile Island covered everything
with brick dust and made the sky and cows
piebald.
Do I matter?
No, of course not.
The mice did.
No, I'm sorry. They meant nothing.
What do I mean?
You mean, do I *really* matter?
Why am I angry?
It's hot, fool, and the Blatz tastes like brick
dust and made the sky and
cows piebald and you don't matter and
the mice don't matter and you're beginning
to realize that nothing *really* matters and
you're pissed.
Why am I angry?
Oh. It's really quite simple, isn't it?
No, I'm sorry, but it's all rather complex.
Then why am I angry?
Because you're pissed. Simple or complex or
why does not matter. You are pissed and
must deal with things on that level.

EARL SIGMUND

2. From the same journal entry select and sequence a poem of your own. How does your felt idea differ from those of Adams, Decker, Heinz, Weber, Bastasic, and Sigmund?

part two

making the poem

THE VALUE OF CONCRETE WORDS

"Scratch, tickle, sting, gasp, shut your eyes, sneeze" or "Discomfort, irritation, severe nasal congestion, explosive expulsion." Which of these series would you understand? Which would you feel in your nose?

"The curtain hung a little crooked, the sofa sagged in the middle, the milk in her glass smelled sour. When she passed the mirror she noticed that her skirt sagged in the back and her hem was down. She was depressed." Do you need the last sentence to know that she was depressed?

Consider the following: "A yard high, a yard and a half long, and ten inches of open mouth with inch-high teeth; four feet by six feet of dark blue uniform; a stick as thick as her wrist with a rough knob at the end." All these could mean *protection*. Would you be willing to use that word instead of *dog, cop*, and *club*? One student said, "I'd say *protection* because I don't protect myself with any of these. I use a thick, locked door." Another said, "I agree. My father keeps a telephone and a brick on his bedside table." And a third added, "We're more afraid of fire. We have a smoke alarm and a fire extinguisher. The word *protection* would cover these too." But one disagreed: "If I wanted to make someone feel protected, I'd have to get him frightened first, really scared, then give him a club or a fierce dog or a cop. Just to say, 'You need protection,' wouldn't scare him enough."

In a way these four students are saying the same thing. They know that the senses perceive only concreteness and send only sensations to the brain. When the brain conceives an idea, it can only combine and extract likenesses, differences, and patterns from those sensations. The *idea* of protection is abstracted from many separate stinks, bangs, splashes, and flashes. To create the *experience* of protection, the poet must find the words that point to the original things. Where the first three students disagreed with the fourth was on which words would point to the largest number of things. The word *protection* does mean many more kinds of protection than *dog, cop*, and *club*. But the fourth student noticed that it didn't mean in quite the same way. She is saying that a single thing will point to many more things than any non-thing can do, even though the non-thing abstracts the main quality common to them all. For an abstract word to work, readers would have to recall, instantly, past experiences of their own in greater detail than they usually carry them in mind. That takes an

3 concreteness and abstraction

effort they may not be able to make or willing to make. Say *protection*, and they may refuse to recall the sound of footsteps in the dark; but say *dog, cop, club*, and they may hear a stair creak and feel a tightening in the throat.

Take another example: Which starts your mouth watering more, "I just filled the refrigerator with fresh fruit. Have some" or "I just peeled a tangerine. Want a bite?" If it puts tangerine on your tongue, its rubberiness, its sting, the sensation of juice squirting, you may be able to imagine a grape there too or a nectarine; you may feel the roundness and firmness of an apple in your left hand and the different firmness of a peach in your right — even hear the sound of seeds plopping in the sink. Even if you prefer grapefruit or have never tasted a tangerine, your jaw, lips, tongue, teeth, hands, eyes, ears, and nose will have started assembling the experience to extract the concept of fresh fruit.

Words that convey this *thingness* or *concreteness* are called *images*. They stand for sensations of sight, sound, taste, touch, smell, and muscle tension. They are the opposite of *abstractions*, which, though they must once have been distilled from things and what things do, no longer have sensory equivalents. For example, *life* vs. *chewing, swallowing, running; peace* vs. *holding out your hand, melting down your gun; hunger* vs. *eating three pizzas in a row*.

EXERCISES

1. The following poem by Denise Levertov has had some of its concreteness removed. Try putting this concreteness back by inserting one of the bracketed words or phrases into each blank space.

WEDDING-RING

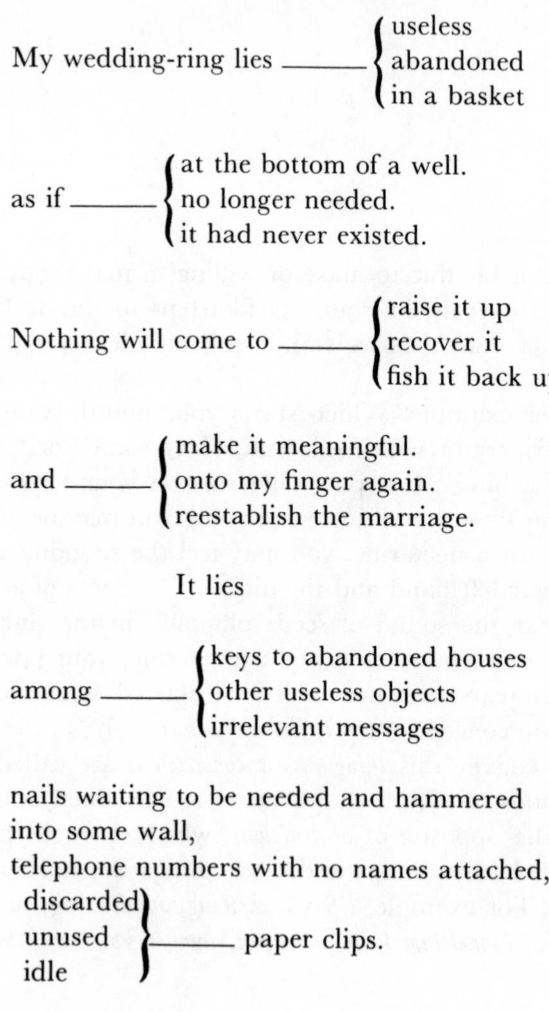

My wedding-ring lies _____ { useless / abandoned / in a basket }

as if _____ { at the bottom of a well. / no longer needed. / it had never existed. }

Nothing will come to _____ { raise it up / recover it / fish it back up }

and _____ { make it meaningful. / onto my finger again. / reestablish the marriage. }

It lies

among _____ { keys to abandoned houses / other useless objects / irrelevant messages }

nails waiting to be needed and hammered
into some wall,
telephone numbers with no names attached,
{ discarded / unused / idle } _____ paper clips.

It can't be given away
for fear of bringing ill-luck.
It can't be sold
for the marriage was good in its own
time, though that time is gone.

Could some ______ { artificer / workman / creator }

beat into it bright stones, transform it

into ______ { ordinary jewelry no one could take / a dazzling circlet no one could take / a multipurpose ring no one could take }

for solemn betrothal or to make promises
living will not let them keep? Change it
into a simple gift I could give in friendship?

2. It has been argued that the following poem would work better without its last line. Do you agree or disagree? Why?

THE JACOB'S LADDER

The stairway is not
a thing of gleaming strands
a radiant evanescence
for angels' feet that only glance in their tread, and need not
touch the stone.

It is of stone.
A rosy stone that takes
a glowing tone of softness
only because behind it the sky is doubtful, a doubting
night gray.

A stairway of sharp
angles, solidly built.
One sees that the angels must spring
down from one step to the next, giving a little
lift of the wings:

and a man climbing
must scrape his knees, and bring
the grip of his hands into play. The cut stone
consoles his groping feet. Wings brush past him.
The poem ascends.

DENISE LEVERTOV

3. Lay on the table a hairbrush, a coconut, an egg, a shoe, a ring, an apple. Handle, smell, look over each one carefully for ten minutes. Choose one and write down anything that suggests itself as you look at it. After two pages or ten minutes of free association, whichever comes first, exchange papers. Determine from the list what the object is and the author's attitude toward it. Select and sequence from the list to make others feel the same way.

THE VALUE OF ABSTRACT WORDS

Should a poem never use abstract words like *fear* and *bliss, label* and *make*? Certainly they are useful in expository prose like this book. Where explanation is the purpose, rather than stimulating feeling, abstraction is an economy. Abstractions can also be useful, even preferable, in poems, *if* you are careful not to substitute the abstraction for the things it was abstracted from. A skillful poet can use abstractions so that they even become things. Consider the following:

Nothing answers to
nothing. Nothing
else. The question
is not how to outlive
life, but how
— in the time we're
possessed by — to face
the raw beauty of being.

PHILIP BOOTH

All the words in this poem are abstract. The most nearly concrete are *raw* and *face*. But though we can see raw meat, we cannot see raw beauty, and to face a situation means only to accept and direct attention to it. How then does Booth manage to create feeling? He does it by making a dramatic situation, with persons reacting to each other. *We* ask *Nothing* a question and it answers. *Time* possesses us as a master possesses slaves. We face a raw beauty of *being*, which includes *human beings*. By making ideas into persons, Booth has made *no thing* into *all things*.

The following poem uses abstractions quite differently but just as successfully:

IN THE SUBURBS

There's no way out.
You were born to waste your life.
You were born to this middleclass life

As others before you
Were born to walk in procession
To the temple, singing.

LOUIS SIMPSON

Stanza 1 is abstract; we see and hear nothing. Stanza 2 is concrete; we see a procession moving toward a temple and hear singing. Simpson is using abstraction here for contrast between our attitude toward our modern suburban life, which we call flat and meaningless, and ancient civilizations, which we think of as dignified and meaningful. He says the two are alike; people are always born into their ways of life. Because he puts the concrete stanza last, in the more emphatic position, he seems to suggest that our middleclass lives seem a dull waste because we are too close to them and too used to them to notice or value their purpose or outline. Perhaps to some future civilization our middleclass lives might look like a procession singing.

EXERCISES

1. Do abstractions work to suggest things in the following poem? How or how not?

UM-M-M-M

Did you do it?
Could you do it?
Will you do it?

Could you hide it?
Would you hide it?
If you told it,

Would it matter?
If it mattered,
Would you falter?

If it fails,
Will you feel
Better?

2. The following poem is concrete except for the title. Would one of the following titles serve better? Why or why not? "Picnic with Thunderstorm," "Fickle Weather," "Sunday, June 12."

DIVINE LOVE

A lip which had once been stolid, now moving
Gradually around the side of the head
Eye-like
The eye twisted on the end of somebody's finger and spinning
Around the sun, its ear,
And the brain aloft over the lake of the face —
Near the cataract of the body —
Like a cumulus cloud enlarged before a rainstorm:

A sound
That grows, gradually, somewhere off to the East
Driving everything before it: cattle and rainbows and lovers

All, all finally swept back

To the table of the body at which five men and two
 women are casually sitting down to eat

MICHAEL BENEDIKT

3. Select and sequence the following list of concrete and abstract terms to create two of the following felt ideas in the reader:

 a. Sensations of smoothness.
 b. A contrast between smoothness and harshness.
 c. A change from comfort to discomfort or vice versa.
 d. A definition of bliss.

 List: *fur, silk, water, milk, cheese, meal, satin, soap, wire, saw, briar, bolt, pleasure, luxury, ease, wealth, pleasant taste, good feel, smooth texture, tactile bliss, rake, file, comb, screen.*
4. From the following abstractions select and sequence about twelve to fifteen so that they say something. Give your grouping a title, but do not tell the class. Invite the class to suggest a title. Do any of theirs come near yours? Invite suggestions for further revisions in your direction or in one of theirs: *think, rely, weigh, plan, measure, scheme, induce, relieve, contrive, cover, remove, deceive, move, modify, discover, comply, imply, move over, decide, provide, recover, apply.*
5. Free associate a page of abstractions of your own. See if you detect any recurrent theme or pattern. Select and sequence to suggest a felt idea. Withhold title and invite class reactions. Revise into a poem.

THE STRUCTURE OF AN IDEA

Draw a raindrop, an arrow, a baseball field. Why are they shaped the way they are? Could they be shaped differently and still function? Can they be mistaken for one another? What is the shape of water pouring from a pitcher? A leaf falling? What is the shape of a journey? The story of a journey? An argument? A choice between two things? A gradual realization?

The raw material of poems comes to you like a box of loose buttons saved for possible future use. But once you discover the *idea*, you will find that it has a structure, that is, a shape of its own. Consider the following poem:

BURNING THE SMALL DEAD

Burning the small dead
          branches
broke from beneath
   thick spreading
               whitebark pine.

               a hundred summers
snowmelt   rock   and air

hiss in a twisted bough.

   sierra granite;
               mt. Ritter —
               black rock twice as old.

Deneb, Altair

windy fire

Gary Snyder

Snyder's idea is that all things are manifestations of a universal substance: fire. The stars are great fires; the rocks and mountains are cooled remains

4 structure

of volcanic fires; the trees have grown with the help of the sun's fire; and the camper is turning them back into fire. History is a burning. The poem is structured to move readers from here, now, the single man, and the single small fire upward, outward, and backward in time — as if we were looking through a funnel from the small end or through a telescope. This is the structure of widening perception. The poet's purpose is to extend and widen our perception of the nature of the universe and our place in it.

The following poem is a prayer, structured as a series of requests, with reasons:

BATTER MY HEART

Batter my heart, three-personed God; for you
As yet but knock, breathe, shine, and seek to mend;
That I may rise and stand, o'erthrow me, and bend
Your force, to break, blow, burn, and make me new.
I, like an usurped town, to another due,
Labor to admit You, but Oh, to no end!
Reason, Your viceroy in me, me should defend,
But is captived, and proves weak or untrue.

Yet dearly I love You, and would be loved fain.
But am betrothed unto Your enemy:
Divorce me, untie, or break that knot again,
Take me to You, imprison me, for I,
Except You enthrall me, never shall be free,
Nor ever chaste, except You ravish me.

John Donne

The poem can be summarized: "Chastise me more severely, Lord, because you're not doing it enough now to make me serve you, whom I wish to serve. You must help because I can't do it for myself." Line 1 makes the request: "Batter my heart." Line 2 gives the reason: "you're not doing it hard enough." Lines 3 and 4 repeat the request: "You must beat me," and give the reason: "in order to strengthen me to serve you better." Lines 5–11 give the reason why God must do it rather than the speaker: "because I am helpless." Lines 11–12 repeat the request: "Overpower me." Lines 13–14 give the reason: "to make me chaste and free, that is, worthy of your service." The structure is familiar to any one who has heard a child ask his father, "Please give me, because...." In this poem God is the father and the speaker is his child. The structure of asking is the same, even though the child is not asking for candy, but for battering, imprisonment, and rape.

In the next poem Stevens implies that placing anything foreign or strange in the center of chaos will focus our attention on it and make us interpret everything else as subordinate.

ANECDOTE OF THE JAR

I placed a jar in Tennessee,
And round it was upon a hill.
It made the slovenly wilderness
Surround that hill.

The wilderness rose up to it,
And sprawled around, no longer wild.
The jar was round upon the ground
And tall and of a port in air.

It took dominion everywhere.
The jar was gray and bare.
It did not give of bird or bush,
Like nothing else in Tennessee.

WALLACE STEVENS

This idea has the same structure as a daisy with button center and surrounding petals, an island surrounded by water, a whirlpool with a spiral movement toward a central hole, or a star or sun with rays. Stevens uses a jar in Tennessee, but it could have been a chair on a hill in West Virginia or a flagpole on the moon. He gives this structure to each of the three stanzas of the poem: In stanza 1 we see the jar in the center and follow its influence out into the wilderness; in stanza 2 we see its influence in the former wilderness and follow it back to the center; in stanza 3 we face the center, staring at the jar, more aware than ever of its difference from and power over its surroundings. The overall structure of the poem is the structure of intensifying awareness. Each stanza enlarges the picture given by the last. In each the jar grows taller and more powerful until what started out as a container for peanut butter or marmalade is now as huge and threatening as a fortified castle or a nuclear power plant. The wilderness of our attention has been drawn and fixed.

THE STRUCTURE OF APPEARANCE

The structure of a poem's felt idea not only controls the order of what it says, but to a lesser extent the way it looks on the page. When you leaf through a book of poems the first thing you notice is the space they take up, how much black in proportion to how much white, how that proportion changes as it moves from left to right, top to bottom. Suppose you see the following:

1.

2.

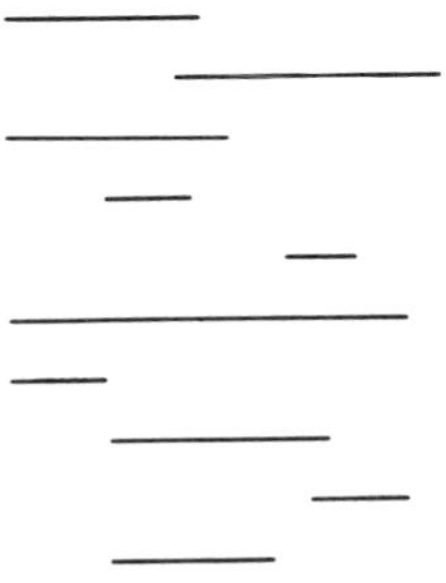

3. **4.** **5.**

Without reading them your reaction might be (1) solemn, dense; heavy reading, perhaps philosophical. (2) Fragmentary, floating; possibly sensations. (3) Thin, tight-lipped, compressed; slight, or makes the reader do most of the work. (4) Wings; must be about rising. Or an hourglass; must be about time. (5) A Christmas tree, probably a greeting card. Your first impression may be wrong, but an expectation has been set up. The poet knows this and is careful to control the effects of that first glance.

Consider the following examples:

1. **SHELL III: ORACLE**

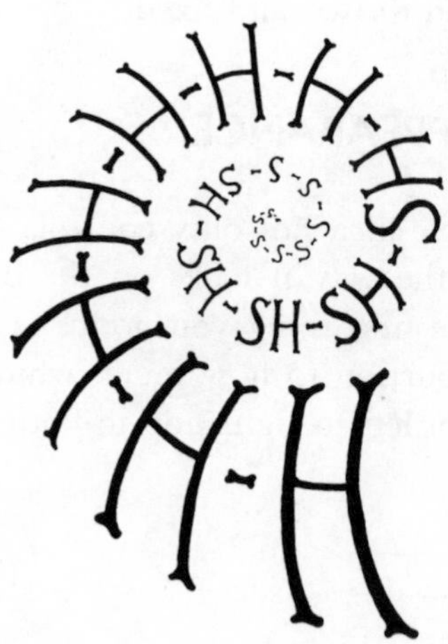

LEONARD TRAWICK

What is an oracle? Does it usually say *sh*? What is a shell for? Is it suitable for an oracle to live in a shell of *sh's*? For what reason might a poet in 1980 label a shell composed of *sh's* "Oracle"?

2. Buffalo Bill 's
defunct
who used to
ride a watersmooth-silver
stallion
and break onetwothreefourfive pigeonsjustlikethat
Jesus

he was a handsome man
and what i want to know is
how do you like your blueeyed boy
Mister Death

e. e. cummings

At first glance, this poem steps from left to right, then steps back. The last line is a two-word name, like the first. And the farthest right line is a one-word name. These names are the only capitalized words in the poem. What shape does this triangle suggest? An arrow? A bullet? At rest or in motion? What relation do the points of the angles have to the life of Buffalo Bill? Is that movement from the left margin to the right an accurate shape for a good life and death? It certainly might be. Buffalo Bill was a famous stage cowboy, with a fantastically good aim at clay pigeons; he has lived, aimed, and ended successfully. Just the shape of the poem on the page suggests that cummings has written a particularly neat tribute. But when you read the words that make up this picture of a speeding bullet, you find a contradiction. The first two lines are irreverent — a sloppy contraction (*Bill's*) and a word for death (*defunct*) that is now used seriously only for things that are lifeless in the first place, like governments, and only jokingly for people. The word *Jesus* here is an expression of admiration for Buffalo Bill's good aim at clay pigeons, not a reference to Christ. The other quality mentioned is his handsome likeness to a blue-eyed boy, not the sign of wisdom and experience we would expect in a seventy-year-old man. And the last two lines address death as "Mister," as one might address a circus manager. The poem seems to ask, "What can one do with a blue-eyed boy who has never grown up? Death is fitting only for the wise and weary who are ready for the spiritual life." This ironic contrast between the speeding-bullet shape of the poem and the spiritual aimlessness of a life spent as a stage cowboy suggests that cummings thinks Buffalo Bill and this way of life are phony.

THE COMPUTER'S FIRST CHRISTMAS CARD

jollymerry
hollyberry
jollyberry
merryholly
happyjolly
jollyjelly
jellybelly
bellymerry
hollyheppy
jollyMolly
marryJerry
merryHarry
hoppyBarry
heppyJarry
boppyheppy
berryjorry
jorryjolly
moppyjelly
Mollymerry
Jerryjolly
bellyboppy
jorryhoppy
hollymoppy
Barrymerry
Jarryhappy
happyboppy
boppyjolly
jollymerry
merrymerry
merrymerry
merryChris
ammerryasa
Chrismerry
asMERRYCHR
YSANTHEMUM

EDWIN MORGAN

"The Computer's First Christmas Card" is spaced on the page so that it looks like a mindless, mechanically randomized printout, as if a computer had been programmed to scramble the words of a greeting card in as many ways as possible. The actual lines, however, make very good sense, as expressions of Christmas cheer slurred increasingly by spiked egg nog. The suggestion that even a computer can be human enough to get drunk at the office Christmas party is not only fun, but a light way of reasserting the humanity that Christmas is all about — or an ironic way of asserting its meaninglessness — or both.

These three are rather obvious examples of the way that the look of a poem reinforces the structure of its felt idea. Their words make actual pictures. You can know part of their meaning without reading them. In most poems the look has a more minor role, yet important enough so that if the poet does not respect it, readers may be misled or distracted on their way to the poet's meaning. In traditional poetry, when you see a chunky shape of fourteen lines, you can expect the internal structure of a sonnet: a question answered, a statement illustrated, an effect preceded or followed by its causes. You can expect a piece of logical thought that is firmly concluded. When you see pages of sonnet-length lines broken into paragraphs instead of stanzas, you can look for narrative. When you see short stanzas of irregular line lengths, you can look for a song. When you see very short poems whose lines are much the same length, you can brace for a witty sting. Not that the visual form is a sure sign, but poets know that if they use a straight left margin and write in lines of certain length clumped in certain ways, readers may recognize a traditional *kind* (*genre*) and may expect the subjects and themes that they have seen in other examples of that genre.

Contemporary poetry is more often written in *open forms*, whose look on the page varies with the shape of each felt idea. Therefore, leafing through a contemporary anthology will show fewer familiar shapes with built-in expectations and more whose function can be recognized only by reading the poems. Both kinds of look give the skillful poet great freedom, but they are different kinds of freedom. The first is like inviting an artist to paint a moustache on the Mona Lisa or to paint a lovelier and more mysterious Mona Lisa of his own. The second requires him to paint a lady so uniquely his own that her beauty has never yet been seen or imagined. Poets who use an open form run both a greater risk of failure and a greater chance of success, a greater risk that readers may not understand them, and a greater chance that their unique shapes on the page may be the only shapes that can perfectly embody their unique ideas.

Consider how Gary Snyder took the risk and the chance in "Song of the Taste":

SONG OF THE TASTE

Eating the living germs of grasses
Eating the ova of large birds

the fleshy sweetness packed
around the sperm of swaying trees

The muscles of the flanks and thighs of
soft-voiced cows
the bounce in the lamb's leap
the swish in the ox's tail

Eating roots grown swoll
inside the soil

Drawing on life of living
clustered points of light spun
out of space
hidden in the grape.

Eating each other's seed
eating
ah, each other.

Kissing the lover in the mouth of bread:
lip to lip.

GARY SNYDER

The poem has nineteen separate lines: eight begin on the left margin; six others are indented slightly; and five are indented considerably more. The lines occur in six unevenly sized and shaped groups that suggest stanzas. Each of these begins with a capital in the left margin and ends, with one exception, on a line that starts with the first or second indentation. The overall effect is that of starting at the left and drifting toward the right, starting again at the left and drifting again toward the right. Why does Snyder want the reader to move in that manner? Partly, I think, because he wants his idea to dawn on his reader gradually, as it would on a person who was in the process of discovering the idea for himself. The poem begins as a list of foods. The lines that begin the first three groups list seed, eggs, nuts, parts of animals, and roots. We accept these. We have them on our grocery lists. The indented lines expand these into the complete beings of which they are parts: the nuts into swaying trees; the muscles of flanks and thighs into the soft voices of cows, the lamb's leap, and the ox-tail's swish; the root into a fetus inside a pregnant earth's womb. These are less easy to accept. We like to think we eat to preserve life, not to destroy it. The fourth group or stanza varies, while preserving, the pattern. It drifts right to describe the living source, then returns left to name the food, grapes. The fifth returns to the form of the first, second, and third groups and begins with the same word, *eating*, then drifts right to expand *seed* to *each other*. This is still harder to accept. It makes us cannibals. The sixth and last stanza uses the same form of drifting from general term to its particulars, but this time *eating* has become *kissing*, and the kiss drifts right to become *bread* at the *lip*. The reader, drifting along the current of irregularly spaced lines, has come to the conclusion that eating and being eaten are a natural and necessary joining, a form of love. I think Snyder would have trouble telling us that directly. In this form, a form that lets our eyes and thoughts drift along, we seem to *come to* the conclusion rather than be *confronted* by it.

EXERCISES

1. What expectations does the appearance on the page of each of the following create? How have the poets conformed to or contradicted each expectation to create their felt ideas?

JOY SONNET IN A RANDOM UNIVERSE

Sometimes I'm happy: la la la la la la la
la la la la la la la la la la la la la la la la
la la la la. Tum tum ti tum. La la la la la la
la la la la la la la la la la la la la la la la.
Hey nonny nonny. La la la la la la la la
la la la la la la la la la la la. Vo do di o do.
Poo poo pi doo. La la la la la la la la la
la la la la la la la la la la la la la la la la
la la. Whack a doo. La la la la la la. Sh-
boom, sh-boom. La la la la la la la la la
la la la la la la la la la la la la la la la la
la la. Dum di dum. La la la la la la la la
la la la la la la la la la. Tra la la. Tra la la
la la la la la la la la la la. Yeah yeah yeah.

HELEN CHASIN

NUNS FRET NOT

Nuns fret not at their convent's narrow room;
And hermits are contented with their cells;
And students with their pensive citadels;
Maids at the wheel, the weaver at his loom,
Sit blithe and happy; bees that soar for bloom,
High as the highest Peak of Furness-fells,
Will murmur by the hour in foxglove bells:
In truth the prison, unto which we doom
Ourselves, no prison is: and hence for me,
In sundry moods, 'twas pastime to be bound
Within the sonnet's scanty plot of ground;
Pleased if some souls (for such there needs must be)
Who have felt the weight of too much liberty,
Should find brief solace there, as I have found.

WILLIAM WORDSWORTH

2. Does the following poem adequately create the feeling of loneliness for you? If so, why? If not, how would you change its look to suggest loneliness more accurately?

l(a

l(a

le
af
fa

ll

s)
one
l

iness

3. The following clump of words gives the words in their original order, but not in their original shape on the page. Arrange them in such a way that the appearance on the page represents the felt idea.

The sky was candy
luminous
edible
spry pinks
shy lemons
greens
chocolates.
Under, a locomotive
spouting violets.

4. In the following poem substitute a word for each picture. Why do you think the author used the pictures?

SUNDAY MORNINGS

LONG AGO, WHEN POPEYE FELT 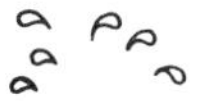
AND THE BLUE GOON SAID, 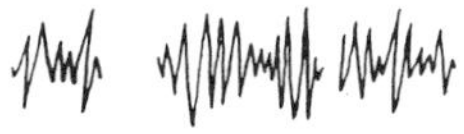
AND INTO SWEE' PEA'S MIND FLASHED 
THEN !! 
AND GEEZIL SLUNK OFF MUTTERING # @ !! 
—MY DADDY READ THE FUNNIES SO 
(EVEN WHEN HIS BREATH 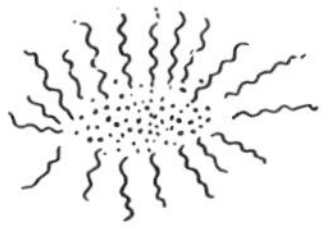)
—HE WAS  , IT WAS REALLY 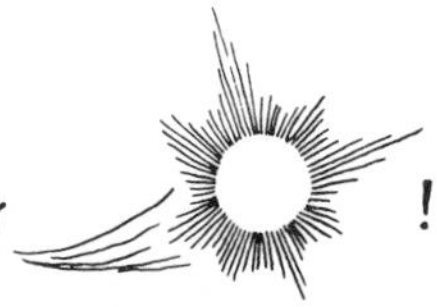 !
AND EVEN NOW, THOUGH MY DAYS  ,
MY BREAD  , AND MY BEER  ,
IN SPITE OF  ,  , AND  ,
WHEN I OPEN THOSE SUNDAY FUNNIES, !

(*Continued*)

LEONARD TRAWICK

5. In each of the following poems what is the felt idea? How has the poet structured (shaped) the poem to help create the idea?

THIRTEEN WAYS OF LOOKING AT A BLACKBIRD

I

Among twenty snowy mountains,
The only moving thing
Was the eye of the blackbird.

II

I was of three minds,
Like a tree
In which there are three blackbirds.

III

The blackbird whirled in the autumn winds.
It was a small part of the pantomime.

IV

A man and a woman
Are one.
A man and a woman and a blackbird
Are one.

V

I do not know which to prefer,
The beauty of inflections,
Or the beauty of innuendoes,
The blackbird whistling
Or just after.

VI

Icicles filled the long window
With barbaric glass.
The shadow of the blackbird
Crossed it, to and fro.
The mood
Traced in the shadow
An indecipherable cause.

VII

O thin men of Haddam,
Why do you imagine golden birds?
Do you not see how the blackbird
Walks around the feet
Of the women about you?

VIII

I know noble accents
And lucid, inescapable rhythms;
But I know, too,
That the blackbird is involved
In what I know.

IX

When the blackbird flew out of sight,
It marked the edge
Of one of many circles.

X

At the sight of blackbirds
Flying in a green light,
Even the bawds of euphony
Would cry out sharply.

XI

He rode over Connecticut
In a glass coach.
Once, a fear pierced him,
In that he mistook
The shadow of his equipage
For blackbirds.

XII

The river is moving.
The blackbird must be flying.

XIII

It was evening all afternoon.
It was snowing
And it was going to snow.
The blackbird sat
In the cedar-limbs.

WALLACE STEVENS

ARIEL[1]

Stasis in darkness.
Then the substanceless blue
Pour of tor and distances.

God's lioness,
How one we grow,
Pivot of heels and knees! — the furrow

Splits and passes, sister to
The brown arc
Of the neck I cannot catch,

Nigger-eye
Berries cast dark
Hooks —

Black sweet blood mouthfuls,
Shadows.
Something else

Hauls me through air —
Thighs, hair;
Flakes from my heels.

[1] *Ariel*: The name of Sylvia's saddle horse and the name of a spirit in Shakespeare's *The Tempest.*

White
Godiva, I unpeel —
Dead hands, dead stringencies.

And now I
Foam to wheat, a glitter of seas.
The child's cry

Melts in the wall.
And I
Am the arrow,

The dew that flies
Suicidal, at one with the drive
Into the red

Eye, the cauldron of morning.

SYLVIA PLATH

6. Sit in front of a basin or puddle of water for fifteen minutes to half an hour. Write two pages of literal details and random words and phrases that come to you while you're doing this. Put the raw material aside overnight. What shape is the resulting idea? Select and sequence to reveal this shape. Do the same in front of a mirror or a windowpane with raindrops or snowflakes pelting it or under a sky of moving clouds or before a pot of boiling water or soup.
7. Take one of the following ideas that you believe in, but which is so familiar in the media that everyone is sick of hearing about it: *Clean air; Industrial pollution kills fish; Black is beautiful; women's rights; the right to life; War is not good for children and other living things*; or any other similar overfamiliar expression. Put it at the top of a piece of paper and put down whatever random remarks occur to you in the space of ten minutes or two pages. Select the ten to fifteen of these random remarks that seem to create your attitude toward the subject. Arrange these in both an internal and an external structure that express your attitude. (You may use a traditional or an open form or a picture.) Remove the original heading and see if the class can suggest a title that points to both your subject and your attitude.
8. Do the same as in 7 for one of the following abstractions: *balance, money, glitter, trash, embarrassment, "cool."*

You're stamping your foot or shovelling snow or sneezing. In what parts of your body do you notice these actions? If you were to notate them by ´ for movements of effort and ˘ for intervals of less effort and a blank space for rest, stamping would be represented by ´´´´, shovelling snow by ´˘ ´˘ ´˘ ´˘, and sneezing by ˘´ ˘´ ˘´ ˘´. These notations record only four stamps, four shovelfuls, and four sneezes. Would these patterns be the same for ten of each? Fourteen? Why? The recurrence of effort, movement, or sound at regular intervals is called *rhythm.* Because spoken words occur in the ear as sounds at intervals, written words, even if not read aloud, occur in the mind's ear as sounds at intervals too. The English language, unlike Chinese or Latin, occurs as a series of *stressed* and *unstressed* syllables (*heavy, light* or *accented, unaccented*). English poetry and prose, therefore, are heard primarily as stresses, with accompanying, subordinate unstressed sounds. These may occur naturally, as the result of language structure and meaning (Pleáse gĕt úp ănd shŭt thĕ dóor) or as the result of intense emotion (Ĭ'm láme, Ĭ'm lóst. Whў mé?) or to represent physical motion (Úp ănd dówn ănd báck ănd fórth ănd ín ănd óut ŏf thĕ sún wĕnt thĕ swíng). Or rhythm may be specially designed by a speaker or writer to create an emotion, a physical sensation, or a felt idea.

EXERCISES

1. Watch the pulse in your wrist or feel your breathing or chew something or swing your foot. Choose one of these and write down its rhythm in stress and nonstress symbols until you have that rhythm firmly fixed in your ear. Now continue writing the rhythm, but with random words instead of the stress symbols. Continue for two pages or ten minutes, whichever comes first. Exchange papers and see if any pattern of feeling or felt idea has surfaced. Select and sequence to reveal that pattern. Or select and sequence your own list and ask the class to suggest a title.
2. Free associate in the rhythm of "Eeny, meeny, miney, mo." After two pages or ten minutes exchange papers and see what self-portrait each student's list has drawn of him or her. Select, sequence, and title or reveal that portrait. Return to author. If author is willing, discuss with class.
3. Free associate to a familiar tune whose words you don't know or have forgotten or mostly forgotten. A hymn or nursery rhyme or other sim-

5 rhythm

ple rhythm would be best. After ten minutes or two pages look for traces of a felt idea, then select and sequence to reveal it and ask the rest of the class to give it a title.

The following remarks by three speakers were heard one morning on a campus elevator:

First speaker: “Hol̓d it̆. Thańks. I’̆m lat́e. Woŭld yŏu pleáse púsh nińe?”
Second speaker: “As̆ Í wăs sáyin̆g ăt th̆e meétin̆g yéster̆day̆, tŏ cút th̆e ădmínis̆trătiv̆e búdgĕt nów woŭld sér̆ioŭsly̆ thŕeatĕn —”
Third speaker: “Laśt stóp. His̆tŏry̆, ph̆ilósŏphy̆, rĕlígiŏn, déan’s of́fic̆e. Bé pr̆epaŕed tŏ meét yoŭr fáte.”
First speaker: “Oút, pleáse.”

This is common prose, in the same language but by different voices for different purposes. The first speaker is in a breathless hurry; the second speaker has already settled down to the day’s business; the third is clowning, being overemphatic on purpose. We know this not only because of what they say but because they speak in the rhythms of their emotional needs. The voice that says, “Hold it. Thanks. I’m late. Would you please push nine? Out please" is tense, already out of breath. Its rhythm is jerky; its accented syllables are heavily stressed. The five sentences are unusually short. Three of the four are commands. The resulting rhythm is as emphatic as machine-gun fire, ´˘ ´ ˘´ ˘˘´´´ ´´. The second speaker's voice is in the rhythm of a leisurely conversation he's begun before getting on the elevator and will continue after he gets off. It's explaining, not commanding. Its seventeen words are only part of a longer sentence. Only ten of its thirty syllables are heavily stressed. The rhythm is ˘´˘´˘˘˘´˘´˘˘˘´˘˘´˘˘˘´˘´˘´˘˘˘˘´˘, a less emphatic rhythm than that of the first voice, with considerably more delay needed to squeeze the unaccented syllables between the accented ones. This speaker is not under tension, has already relaxed into his normal emotional rhythm for the day. The voice that said, "Last stop. History, philosophy, religion, dean's office. Be prepared to meet your fate" is acting, inflating its effect in order to mock. The way it announces that top floor is to exaggerate its importance, to put down the idea of authority. It almost chants. The twenty-two syllables in the thirteen words of its three sentences contain eleven stresses repeated at intervals more regular than usual in prose communication: ´´ ´˘˘˘´˘˘˘´˘´´˘ ´˘´˘´˘´.

Three kinds of rhythmic patterns occur in this speech: stresses with no unstressed syllables in the first sentence; stresses with unstressed syllables in various positions in the second; a regular alternation of heavy and light stresses in the third. As I left the elevator, a student went by singing to herself, "Bóbby̆ Sháftŏe wént tŏ séa/ Hé'll cŏme báck ăńd márr̆y ḿe/Dá d̆a dúmp tĕ dée dĕe dée/ Ṕretty̆ Bóbby̆ Sháftŏe." The lines of the nursery rhyme were in the same ´˘´˘´˘´ rhythm as the "Be prepared to meet your fate" that I'd just heard on the elevator and served the same purpose — to emphasize the feeling already created by the meaning of the words, in this case a confidence that the boy would come back to marry the girl.

The rhythms used by this sequence of voices had just demonstrated the ways that rhythm, in prose or poetry, varies unconsciously in response to emotional needs as the human voice varies in response to the same needs. As plant growth notates seasonal rhythms, the waxing and waning and direction of light notate daily rhythms, and the body's energy notates metabolic rhythms, so speech notates emotional rhythms. The poets' problem is to learn to recognize the rhythms of their own voices when they are intense, relaxed, bored, mocking, and so on, so that their poems will be able to control the reactions of their hearers as their voices do. I say *hearers* because poetry is still publicly performed before live audiences, and the trained readers of printed poetry read it silently as if they were hearing it inside their heads.

EXERCISES

Tape-record or write down the next words you hear on a bus, in the elevator, or in the supermarket. Identify the rhythms by marking the most heavily stressed syllables. What rhythmical patterns occur? In what ways do the rhythms carry emotions?

USING TRADITIONAL RHYTHMS

To illustrate the most obvious way that poets control rhythm to convey their felt ideas, consider the following nursery rhyme:

RING AROUND THE ROSY

Rińg ărouńd tȟe rósy̆
Ă póckĕt fúll oȟ pósiĕs
Tiśhă tiśhă
Wĕ áll fáll dowń

ANONYMOUS

The idea is subordinate to the rhythm in this poem. What it says is not nearly so important as that it directs small children to link hands in a circle and dance around a center, then stop and suddenly sit down. It is a way of organizing toddlers to amuse and control them — a sort of action game. The stresses are regularly spaced in the first three lines, and in the last line the crash is prepared, even ensured, by the clustering of the three stressed syllables in the line together, with no unstressed syllables between. The same use of rhythm to ensure or accompany physical action can be found in work songs, like "The Volga Boatman's Song" or any counting-out song, like "Eeny, Meeny, Miney, Mo."

A somewhat subtler use of traditional rhythms occurs when poets want to play their ideas against expected rhythms by varying them just enough so that a hearer's expectation is disappointed — just a little, not entirely. The rhythmic variation that surprises will emphasize some word or words especially important to what the poet is trying to do. Take

Donne's "Batter My Heart," whose structure we have already examined on page 39: You may have to read the poem several times again before you realize that the basic rhythm is *iambic pentameter*: five groups (feet) of ˘ ´ 's (iambs) to a line. Only lines 10 and 14 preserve that meter exactly. But because the poem is a *sonnet* in the period of the sonnet's greatest popularity, Donne knew that his readers would be expecting fourteen lines of iambic rhythm. The felt idea of the poem, however, and its driving emotion are anything but regular. It is a prayer out of spiritual agony. The speaker is pleading to be whipped, raped, bound, and imprisoned. How can the regularity of iambic rhythm achieve such passion? Donne does it by strategically placed variations. For example, the first line substitutes a ´˘ for the expected ˘´ and places that variation on the word *batter*, which means and sounds like a blow. The second line substitutes a stressed syllable, *breathe*, for the expected unstressed one in the third foot. A list of one-syllable coordinates like *knock, breathe, shine*, and *seek* could not naturally be read ´˘´˘´; meaning, syntax, and punctuation of the series require them to be read with equal stress. The same is true of line 4, where the gentleness and courtesy of the first series is paralleled by the violent actions that the speaker wishes God would substitute. The fifth and sixth lines admit despair and failure in what seems like the rhythm of unmetrical speech: "Í, lĭke ăn ŭsurṕt towńe, tŏ aňótheř dúe,/ Lábŏr tŏ ădmít yŏu, bŭt ó, tŏ nó eńd!" But Donne has chosen just those metrical variations that emphasize his felt idea. He places the accented syllables in positions that underscore pain: *Í, ŭsuŕpt, tówn, lábŏr*, and *Ó, tŏ nó eńd*. If the rhythm were regular, *I, surpt, la-, O*, and *no* would be unaccented. At the end, in line 14, the base rhythm and the idea come together ("Nŏr éveř cháste, ĕxcépt Yŏu rávĭšh mé") to show that the emotion has calmed. Throughout, Donne has adapted iambic pentameter to the rhythm of intense emotion, which moves in gusts.

EXERCISES

1. Find other places in Donne's poem where the intensity of the passion has altered the expected regularity of the meter. How have these changes supported the poet's meaning?
2. Examine two other metered poems in Poems for Further Discussion and try to determine why their authors made specific metrical variations.

USING FREE-VERSE RHYTHMS

Free-verse poems, which are not written in meter, cannot depend on this device of playing the unexpected against the expected rhythm. What the reader of free verse expects is the normal speaking voice modified to suit each felt idea. The results range from rhythms that barely suggest meter to the rhythms of emotional speech. The following poem hints at, though it does not follow, meter:

WHY I'M NOT MAKING MY LAST TRIP NOW

I have nothing to bring
except two empty hands
that once were fists, eyes
that see less each day, eleven
teeth veined with silver
and sadly spaced. My fear
of water, my growing fear
of high winds, of seeing
the earth at great height
and wanting to fall soundlessly
through ages of cold air until
I became cold air and no more.
I have the 7 untested faiths
of the believer. The first that God
was born in January of '28
while it snowed all afternoon
on Pingree Ave. and my fathers
roared. The last that you
will believe me. How can
I go without clean socks?
(My aunt would not buy shoes
without clean socks.) How
can I enter the kingdom
without a hat? How can I
put my luggage in a wish
and whistle the whole way?
How can I make you understand
I'm still foolish and I won't go!

PHILIP LEVINE

This poem has sometimes three stressed syllables to the line, sometimes four. It is in the syntax of normal prose; hence the rhythm is prose, except that the line ends, which come after each third or fourth stressed syllable, break the sentences where normal syntax would not break them, and so give a suggestion of pattern not conformed to. And that hesitancy, that avoidance of predictable rhythm, *is* the rhythm of the hesitation that the poem is about. Levine knows perfectly well that the last trip is inevitable, but is unwilling to accept it; hence the rhythm of straightforward prose, but checked every three or four feet by a line-end pause, as if for every three or four steps forward, he was forced to take one back. In spite of the evasion of rhythmical regularity, there is a more or less straight and narrow march down the page. Were it not for those line ends, the rhythm of prose syntax would dominate.

If the rhythm of Levine's poem is speech restricted by the memory of meter, the rhythm of the following poem is speech restricted only by the poet's arrangement of stresses and pauses for emphasis.

NIGHT

In the lamplight falling
on the wh́ite táblĕclóth
my plate,
my shining loaf of quietness.

I sit down.
Through the open door
all the absent who I love enter
and we eat.

PETER EVERWINE

The first stanza is one sentence that sets the whole scene for what happens in the second stanza. Everwine chooses to pause on *falling*, *tablecloth*, *plate*, and *quietness*. *Falling* is structurally important because it focuses our eyes on the center of the scene and emotionally important because it suggests a benediction of comfort and clearness from above. The rhythm of *lámplĭght fállĭng* supports the idea of benediction by following each stressed syllable by a lighter one — a stroking rather than a hitting rhythm. The pause after *tablecloth* is an ellipsis to imply the words *are* or *I see*. The rhythm of *white táblĕcloth*, which puts all three stresses of the line on those words, combines with the line-end pause to emphasize the suggestion of an altar or communion table clothed in white, a suggestion reinforced by *plate*, emphasized by its line-end-and-comma pause, and by the stressed syllables of *shíníñg*, *lóaf*, and *quíĕtnĕss* in the stanza's last line.

In the second stanza a communion takes place. *Ĭ sít dówn* is firm and final, in both meaning and rhythm — ending with two stressed syllables and a period. The next line ends on *door*, the last word in its thought group and the key word for making the reader expect the action that happens next. *Áll thĕ ábsĕnt whó Ĭ lóve éntĕr* ends another complete thought group, ends on another key word for the meaning, and puts the two stressed syllables of *lovĕ énteř* together, so that the rhythmic emphasis of both stress and pause fall on the chief actor and the chief act of the poem. The last line of the poem completes the action with three syllables, the last two stressed and supported by the emphasis of the final pause and the period. The communion table has been lighted and laid. The human presence waits, the spiritual presences enter, and they break bread together. To divide any of these lines in different places would create different rhythms and different emphases and might well hinder the poet's clarity and strength.

EXERCISES

The following three poems are in quite different free-verse rhythms. Ask yourself the following questions about them:

1. Which are the stressed and unstressed syllables?
2. What syntactical units is the poet using?
3. How do the line ends and stanza or paragraph breaks work with or against the syntax to help create the felt idea in each poem?

MEETING MY CLASS CALLED "EASY WRITER"

Where the cages were the animals
come back. They lie down to make
the walls be there again. If only
birds could call and make that same
ribbon through the windows!
But there is no way for far
to climb to its old place.

Here in the center we wait, or we
walk back and forth trying to measure
what created the space inside the bars.
Remember when we were failing? Remember
the dungeon that led to the long, bright
day? Now we are hidden in these selves.
The animals are hunting us and we can't
learn how to be found.

WILLIAM STAFFORD

THE FIRST DAYS

optima dies prima fugit[1]

The first thing I saw in the morning
Was a huge golden bee ploughing
His burly right shoulder into the belly
Of a sleek yellow pear
Low on a bough.
Before he could find that sudden black honey
That squirms around in there
Inside the seed, the tree could not bear any more.
The pear fell to the ground
With the bee still half alive
Inside its body.
He would have died had I not knelt down
And sliced the pear gently
A little more open.
The bee shuddered, and returned.
Maybe I should have left him alone there
Drowning in his own delight.
The best days are the first
To flee.

JAMES WRIGHT

[1] Translated by the last two lines.

CALLED

Digging the grave
through black dirt,
gravel and rocks
that will hold her down,
we speak of her heat
which has driven her out
over the highway
in her first year.

A fly glides from her mouth
as we take her four legs,
and the great white neck
mudded at the lakeside
bends gracefully into the arc
of her tongue, colorless, now,
and we set her in the bed
of earth and rock
which will hold her as the sun
sets over her shoulders.

You had spoken of her brother,
100 lbs or more,
and her slight frame
from the diet of chain
she had broken;
on her back
as the spade cools her brow
with black dirt, rocks,
sand, white tongue,
what pups does she hold
that are seeds unspayed
in her broken body;
what does her brother say
to the seed gone out over
the prairie, on the hunt
of the unreturned:
and what do we say
to the master of the dog dead,

heat, highway, this bed
on the shoulder
of the road west
where her brother called, calls.

Michael Harper

USING PROSE RHYTHMS

At the opposite extreme from metered poetry is prose poetry, which is printed as prose and whose line ends are determined by the printer, not the poet. Its rhythm is determined by sentence structure, which poets manipulate carefully to create the same emotional emphases and fluctuations that they could create by meter with substitutions or by speech rhythms with line-end pauses. Consider the following:

IN THE FOREST

I was combing some long hair coming out of a tree. I had noticed the comb on the ground by the roots; the long hair coming out of the tree. The hair and comb seemed to belong together. Not so much that the hair needed combing, but perhaps that reassurance of the comb drawn through it.

I stood in the gloom and silence that many forests have in the pages of fiction, combing the thick womanly hair, the mammal-warm hair, even as the evening slowly took the forest into night.

Russell Edson

The poem's felt idea is to create a sensation of stroking, an emotion of comfort. It is a universal physical and psychological need that small children often satisfy by stroking the satin edge of a blanket or a plush animal's ear. Edson tells the experience as a dream or fairy tale, with an appropriately soothing rhythm, like a sustained drone. He makes this rhythm by repeating words and syntax: The structure of the first sentence and the first part of the second are the same: subject, verb, object, followed by a phrase or phrases; and they are about the same length. The second part of the second sentence is a shortened repetition of the first sentence. The third sentence is a simple sentence like the first and about the same length. The fourth sentence is twice as long, but the strong break before *but* almost makes it two, each about the same length as the first. These structural similarities are reinforced by the repetition of *long hair coming out of a tree*, essentially twice, *hair*, four times, some form of *comb*, five times, and *coming*, which has the same rhythm and almost the same sound[2] as *combing*, twice.

The result of these structural similarities and verbal repetitions is that within and between some of these units there is a rhythmic resemblance unusual in prose. For instance, "Ĭ wăs cómbiňg soḿe lońg háir cómiňg oút ŏf ă trée" (one clause and one phrase, three stresses in each, three of those preceded by two unstressed syllables, ˘˘´). "Ĭ hăd nóticĕd thĕ cońb oň thĕ grouńd bў thĕ roóts" (one clause and two phrases, the ˘˘´ combination repeated four more times.) "Thĕ eńeniňg slówlў toók thĕ fórešt ińtŏ night" (one clause and one phrase; six pairs of ˘´ in a row). "Thĕ háir aňd cońb seémed tŏ bĕlońg" (four groups of one stressed and one unstressed syllable, three of the four in ˘´ pattern, and the second and fourth stresses on words that sound so much alike that they break the clause into rhythmical halves).

Many prose poems have less regular rhythm than Edson's. Some have more. But all prose poets are expected to control rhythm to help create their felt ideas. A successful prose poem cannot be confused rhythmically with an interoffice memo or an article in a medical journal or a social worker's case histories.

EXERCISES

1. Divide the following into lines and stanzas or verse paragraphs to emphasize the felt idea of each. Which one or ones would, in your opinion, be harmed least if left as printed here?

[2] In the use of language, meaning and rhythm and sound cannot be separated, though for purposes of analysis they must be. Edson's sounds reinforce the sustained drone of his rhythm.

a.

Ink runs from the corners of my mouth. There is no happiness like mine. I have been eating poetry. The librarian does not believe what she sees. Her eyes are sad and she walks with her hands in her dress. The poems are gone. The light is dim. The dogs are on the basement stairs and coming up. Their eyeballs roll, their blond legs burn like brush. The poor librarian begins to stamp her feet and weep. She does not understand. When I get on my knees and lick her hand, she screams. I am a new man. I snarl at her and bark. I romp with joy in the bookish dark.

b.

Reliquaries the size of samovars holding bits of the true cross, so crusted over with gold and jewels you'd never notice the toothpick of holy wood if it weren't smack in the center, takes you back to faith in miracles, times they'd pray to that fragment of Calvary, how he got there, from planing wood in the shop, pushing off the long fragrant curls, the shavings, the sawdust that got in your hair and stung your nose, the fresh droplets of sap on the cut tree, sticky as honey and bright as amber, that's memory, a fly trapped forever like a star in a sapphire, night sky over the olive grove at Gethsemane, he put his hand on the trunk, called for his father, I called, stacking wood until my arms were frozen, loading it in the old horse trailer, my father swinging the angry buzz saw, I got a sliver in my palm, cried, we went home with wood, burned it all winter, the glowing logs eaten away by flame, an incandescent heart that looked like miniature cities sacked and smoldering, that's memory, wood, the stick in your hand you smack the sheep with and yell at the dogs, we were there, that's memory, the wood that goes into your house, this paper, his cross, the cedar chest of a bride who is buried in a box of pine.

c.

Which way I fly is Hell; myself am Hell; and in the lowest deep a lower deep still threat'ning to devour me opens wide, to which the Hell I suffer seems a Heav'n. O then at last relent: is there no place left for Repentance, none for Pardon left? None left but by submission; and that word disdain forbids me, and my dread of shame.

d.

Setting a trotline after sundown if we went far enough away in the night sometimes up out of deep water would come a secret-headed channel cat. Eyes that were still eyes in the rush of darkness, flowing feelers noncommittal and black, and hidden in the fins those rasping bone daggers, with one spiking upward on its back. We would come at daylight and find the line sag, the fishbelly gleam and the rush on the tether: to feel the swerve and the deep current which tugged at the tree roots below the river.

e.

Protection, of a kind, was what he was after, and the poetry he invented was easy to understand; he knew human folly like the back of his hand, and was greatly interested in armies and fleets; when he laughed, respectable senators burst with laughter, and when he cried the little children died in the streets.

2. Analyze the function of rhythm in the following poems from Poems for Further Discussion: "anyone lived in a pretty how town" and "if everything happens that can't be done," by e. e. cummings; "The Waking," by Theodore Roethke; "Matter," by Philip Booth; "The Egg," by W. S. Merwin.
3. Write a song in strict meter for an action game for small children, such as jumping rope, licking popsicles, putting on clothes, washing hands.

   OR

   Write a work song for a job you can do in unison with other people, such as hauling in a net, picking fruit, loading a truck, shovelling snow or gravel.
4. Take one of the poems you have written from free association in this course so far. Revise its rhythm to better support its felt idea. Revise another one that you have written, in a different rhythm.
5. Free associate to a metrical pattern for two pages or ten minutes, whichever comes first (don't use rhyme). See if a felt idea has surfaced, then revise, varying the meter for useful emphasis.

Sit very quietly, relax, and breathe deeply and slowly. Where do you feel your breathing? What intervals are there between breathing in and breathing out? In what rhythm do you breathe? Now put *sounds* to your breaths, not words, just the nearest sounding syllables you can make up. It would be harder to put *words* of equally accurate rhythm and sound to breathing. You could say

1. in/out, in/out, in/out.
2. inhale/exhale, inhale/exhale, inhale/exhale.
3. inspiration/expiration, inspiration/expiration, inspiration/expiration.

They would all represent three complete breaths, but only 1 is in the rhythm of real breathing. It would take four jerks of effort to breathe in the rhythm of 2 and eight in the rhythm of 3. And the acutal sound of air passing through nostrils is reproduced by none of them.

In giving information, when the listeners are poised to catch factual meaning instead of feeling, they will probably not notice or care whether rhythm and sound have been selected to make meaning more exact or even whether they work against it. A doctor would need only to hear, "The patient is breathing easily," or, "Her respiration is normal." But a poem is so compressed and so dependent on sensation to create feeling that the rhythm and sound of its words may make the difference between vagueness and clarity. How is a poet to select and sequence the sounds of words so that they reinforce both rhythm and meaning, yet avoid drawing too much attention to themselves as aural tricks?

A poet can use the sounds of English words in three ways:

1. Some words describe sounds by using those sounds (*hum, twitter, roar, moan, wail, quack, crack, crash, thump*, etc.). They are *onomatopoetic*. But even words for sounds often sound unlike those sounds (*sob, hammer, saw, laugh, silence*), and some words of similar sound have contradictory meanings (*thick/thin, sleep/leap, quick/sick, well/ill*).
2. All words use consonant sounds that in themselves and in combination are more or less explosive, fricative, or otherwise impeded in the mouth, and vowel sounds that take a longer or shorter time to say. These separate letter sounds and their combinations have slightly onomatopoetic meanings: Long vowels and diphthongs, as in *peace, doom, call, paid, rope*, are prolonging sounds associated with slow movements and solemn emotions. Short vowels, as in *sit, cat, pet, top, up*, take less time to say and are associated with speed of

6 sound

action and lightness of feeling. Consonants that impede vowel sounds explosively or abrasively, as in *stick, catch, budge, hoist, risk*, are associated with force and anger; consonants whose sounds end a word by leaving it, rather than by snapping it shut, sustain a long vowel even longer (*moan, palm, bale, lure*) and prolong a short vowel (*sum, tell, sin*). Their sounds suggest anything done easily or smoothlv and a mood of comfort or pleasure. But sounds cannot defy meaning or language structure. The word *disease* does not suggest pleasure just because it has the sounds of *please* and *ease*. *Sitch* is not a possible spelling for *sin* just because the meaning of *sin* might seem to demand a harsher sound.

3. Most words are not onomatopoetic nor do they use their vowels and consonants to reinforce their meanings, but long use has often associated their sounds with their meanings so closely that other words having the same sounds may reinforce those meanings, even when their own meanings are contradictory or unconnected. Light has no sound, yet because the word *light* has one, its meaning could be supported not only by *right, might, bright, sight, delight*, which also support the meaning of *light*, but by *blight, fight, bite*, and *slight*, whose meanings move in the opposite direction. Likewise, the feeling of gladness has no sound, but the word *glad* could

be supported in the right context by the same sounds in *sad, bad, mad*, or *cad*. And thinness has no sound, but *thin* could be supported by any short *i*, as in *bit, little, bitter, twitch, skip, hit, miss, tin, bin*. Only *slim* would both sound and mean the same as *thin*.

The best that poets can do with such intractable language is to repeat the sounds that occur in the key words that create their moods and meanings, when they can do it without choosing a grossly abnormal word, distorting syntax, or deforming the felt idea. Consider how sound works in these examples:

Jáck aňd Jiĺl wĕnt uṕ tȟe hiĺl
tŏ fetćh ă páil ŏf wátĕr.
Jaćk fĕll dowń aňd bróke hiš crówn
aňd J́ill căme tuḿbliňg áftĕr.

As a nursery rhyme that will be spoken more often than read and that must catch the brief attention of two- and three-year-olds and amuse them, the poem needs especially obvious rhythm and sound repetitions. The four lines are in ´˘´˘ rhythm, alternating four and three stresses to a line. The meter is about as regular as meter gets. The line ends fall at the ends of thought and syntax groups, the second and fourth accented syllables in lines 1 and 3 rhyme,[1] as do the last words of lines 2 and 4 (probably an exact rhyme when the poem was written) Their rhyme emphasizes not only the regularity of the meter, but key words that indicate *how* and *where, who* and *what*. The names of the two characters begin with the same letter. This emphasizes their sameness — age, purpose, date. The names and their sounds are each repeated, in the same order, at the beginning of lines 3 and 4, as fitting emphasis on the central characters of the story. Are the sound repetitions really important? Try a paraphrase:

Dick and Jane went up the hill
to fetch a pail of water.
Jane fell down and bumped her head
and Dick came tumbling down too.

[1] **Exact rhyme**: identical vowel and final consonant sounds in a word's accented syllable and those that follow (mine/fine, miner/finer, mine/refine).
Slant rhyme:
Alliteration: repetition of words' initial sounds: any vowels (ask/ate/it/even) or the same consonants (feel/fade).
Assonance: identity of accented vowel sounds (feel/peak, wader/failing).
Consonance: identity of final consant sounds (eat/mate, revise/daze, more/rubber).

It's still a poem. The story is the same as well as the concreteness and the rhythm. But the sound no longer emphasizes the characters' names so much, no longer divides lines 1 and 3 into halves containing thought and syntactical units, nor emphasizes the ends of lines 2 and 4, which also mark off thought and syntactical units. In other words, it is not so easy to dance to, listen to, or remember.

The following more sophisticated poem also depends on repeated sounds to emphasize its thought groups and key words. In addition, it uses sound to create a tone (feeling) that moves from playful to forlorn:

WISH FOR A YOUNG WIFE

My lizard, my lively writher,
May your limbs never wither,
May the eyes in your face
Survive the green ice
Of envy's mean gaze;
May you live out your life
Without hate, without grief,
And your hair ever blaze,
In the sun, in the sun,
When I am undone,
When I am no one.

THEODORE ROETHKE

All the words in the first line are slant rhymed: *My* with *lively* and *writher; lizard* with *lively*, and with *limbs* and *wither* in the second line. *Lizard* and *lively writher* both mean swift smoothness, and their sounds move swiftly and smoothly in the ear. Both they and the other words in those two lines begin with the least impeded consonant sounds (*m, l, r, n, w*, and the semivowel *y*), and all but one end with an unimpeded consonant sound (*r*) or one pronounced with only a slight buzz (*mbs*) or with the semivowel *y*. The stressed vowels in these two lines are all long or short *i*, a vowel associated often with both the sounds and meanings of the words *light* and *quick*. Lightness and quickness are also suggested by the rhythm of the key words *lizard, lively, writher, never*, and *wither*, a greater concentration of two-syllable words and thus of lightly stressed syllables than anywhere else in the poem. Meaning, sound, and rhythm have worked together to give the sensory effect of a wriggle and the emotional effect of playful ease.

In contrast, the meaning of the last three lines changes from bright hair blazing in the sun to an old man withered in the sun, and again sounds work with rhythm to emphasize that change. The rhythm has slowed from three stressed syllables and five unstressed in line 1 to five stressed and no unstressed in lines ten and eleven. The sounds have also slowed. Four of the stressed syllables are exact rhymes (*sun, sun, undone, one*), five more share the final *n* sound, and two more share the similar final *m* sound. The dominant vowel sound has shifted from the long and short *i*'s associated with *light* and *quick*, to the short *u* associated with *drum* and *hum*. Since a final *m* or *n* prolongs any vowel that precedes it, even a short vowel like the *u* in *sun*, the words *sun* or *done* would take or seem to take longer to say than *lively or wither*, even though they are shorter words with fewer syllables. Therefore, the shift from *lively* to *sun, writher* to *-done*, and *wither* to *one* sounds like the sensory shift from a flute to a drum and the emotional shift from play to foreboding.

The end-rhyme pattern of the poem has undergone a similar change. The first seven lines end on slant rhymes spaced inconsistently, suggesting that the young wife is too quick and lithe to be restrained by anything as stiff as exact rhymes. But the last three lines end on an exact rhyme, which sounds like a drum beat and emphasizes the contrast between the old husband's slow stiffening and his young wife's limber writhing.

USING SOUND IN TRADITIONAL POETRY

Most traditional poetry depends on patterns of rhymes, as it does on patterns of rhythms. Poetic skill is measured by how well these are varied to suit the needs of each felt idea. The following poem, for example, is a curse on a religious and political enemy, in the form of an Italian sonnet.[2]

ON THE LATE MASSACRE IN PIEDMONT[3]

Avenge, O Lord, thy slaughtered saints, whose bones
Lie scattered on the Alpine mountains cold;
Ev'n them who kept thy truth so pure of old,

[2] *Sonnet*: Fourteen iambic pentameter lines rhyming abab, cdcd, efef, gg (Shakespearean sonnet) or abba, abba, and most often cdecde (Italian sonnet).

[3] The Easter, 1655, massacre of the Waldensian Protestants by the army of the Catholic Duke of Savoy in the Piedmont area of northwestern Italy.

When all our fathers worshiped stocks and stones,
Forget not: in thy book record their groans
Who were thy sheep, and in their ancient fold
Slain by the bloody Piedmontese, that rolled
Mother with infant down the rocks. Their moans
The vales redoubled to the hills, and they
To Heav'n. Their martyred blood and ashes sow
O'er all th' Italian fields, where still doth sway
The triple Tyrant:[4] that from these may grow
A hundredfold who, having learnt thy way,
Early may fly the Babylonian woe.[5]

JOHN MILTON

Note how the long vowel *o* is used onomatopoetically to sound like a howl or moan (*O Lord*), also in words that suggest pain and anger (*bones, cold,* and *woe*), and finally in words that would neither mean nor sound like anger and grief in another context (*sow, grow, fold, rolled*). Note also that although the rhyme scheme of the Italian sonnet is usually *abba abba cdecde*, in this one the last six lines rhyme *cdcdcd* and the *a, b,* and *d* contain the same stressed *o*. The only really different rhyme sound is the *ay* of *they, sway,* and *way,* but even that is a long, extended vowel unstopped by end consonants, like the continuation of a howl or cry. The whole poem is only three sentences, two of which end inside the lines, so that the sustained howl of the repeated *o*'s is emphasized by the ends of the lines rather than broken by them. Inside the lines the long *o* sound of *O Lord* is strategically placed in line 1, where it is read as one of three consecutive stressed syllables, and in the last two lines it is stressed in *hundredfold* and *Babylonian.*

USING SOUND IN FREE VERSE AND PROSE POETRY

Free verse, too, and prose poems use sound repetitions to emphasize felt ideas, though usually, except for humor, they use sounds less conspicuously than metered verse does. William Stafford has said that every syllable rhymes with every other syllable more than with no syllable. He is using the word *rhyme* in a broader sense even than slant rhyme. He would in-

[4] The Pope.
[5] Protestants in Milton's period in England called the Catholic Church the Whore of Babylon.

clude slighter resemblances among vowel and consonant sounds than complete or partial identity. For example:

AT THE EDGE OF TOWN

Sometimes when clouds float
their shadows make dark fields,
wings that open. Just by looking
we become them. Is there a kingdom
where only the soundless have honor?
Some days, yes. We look up and follow.

WILLIAM STAFFORD

This poem points to an experience of unity with the natural world so commonplace and so inconspicuous that it is not proclaimed by those who have it, but merely noticed. It happens in silence and is honored by silence. The words of the poem, however, must have sound. Thus, writing the poem has been an artistic challenge to use sounds to create the feeling of silence. Stafford does this by setting up the ghost of the very emphatic couplet form (a pair of rhymed lines) and proceeding to muffle it. The end words of each of the three pairs of lines have some slant rhymes and some slighter sound resemblances to each other. *Float* and *fields* share the initial *f; looking* and *kingdom* share the *king*, even though it occurs at the beginning of one word and at the end of the other and though one is stressed and the other not; *honor* and *follow* share the stressed short *o*. The first and last final words, *float* and *follow*, share the initial *f* and the long *o*, though only the long *o* in *float* is stressed. The more emphatic end consonants *t* and *ds* of the first couplet, which shocks the grounded with a first awareness of sky, do not occur in any of the four other end words, which end on unstressed syllables and unimpeded consonants, as if Stafford were working away from any sound so decisive and final. Starting on the ground, the speaker has begun to float. And these are only the end sounds of the lines. Inside the lines he supports the initial impact and subsequent sensation of expanding and floating, by moving from stressed syllables with slightly plosive end sounds, like *float, fields, dark, clouds*, to those which hum and hiss and, at their most abrasive, buzz, like *come, them, some, we, wings, days, is, yes, only, follow*. Inside the lines he also repeats sounds that are alike or nearly alike in support of end-line sounds. The stressed *o* of *float* (line 1) appears in the stressed *o's* of *open* (line 3) and *only* (line 5) and in the unstressed *o* of *shadow* (line 2) before moving back to the unstressed *o* of *follow* at the end of the last line. The *ds* of *fields* (line 2) appears in *clouds* (line 1), partly in *wings* (line 3), differently in *soundless* (line 5) and in *days* (line 6), and progressively less harshly. Sometimes a group of words works together to reinforce sounds, as *some days yes* (line 6) reinforces *sometimes* (line 1) and *soundless* (line 5), or *we become them* (line 4) reinforces *wings that open* (line 3) immediately above.

EXERCISES

1. Can you detect other ways that Milton has used sound to reinforce meaning and mood in "On the Late Massacre in Piedmont"?
2. How does the following poem use vowel sounds to vary the expectation of an Italian sonnet's rhyme scheme? How does the poem's felt idea justify this variation?

RANGE-FINDING

The battle rent a cobweb diamond-strung
And cut a flower beside a groundbird's nest
Before it stained a single human breast.
The stricken flower bent double and so hung.
And still the bird revisited her young.
A butterfly its fall had dispossessed,
A moment sought in air his flower of rest,
Then lightly stooped to it and fluttering clung.
On the bare upland pasture there had spread
O'ernight 'twixt mullein stalks a wheel of thread
And straining cables wet with silver dew.
A sudden passing bullet shook it dry.
The indwelling spider ran to greet the fly,
But finding nothing, sullenly withdrew.

ROBERT FROST

3. What is the end-rhyme pattern of the following poem?

ROOT CELLAR

Nothing would sleep in that cellar, dank as a ditch,
Bulbs broke out of boxes hunting for chinks in the dark,
Shoots dangled and drooped,
Lolling obscenely from mildewed crates,
Hung down long yellow evil necks, like tropical snakes.
And what a congress of stinks!
Roots ripe as old bait,
Pulpy stems, rank, silo-rich,
Leaf-mold, manure, lime, piled against slippery planks.
Nothing would give up life:
Even the dirt kept breathing a small breath.

THEODORE ROETHKE

How and where has the poet varied his rhyme scheme? Do you think that these variations have reinforced the poet's felt idea? How? What internal support has the poet given to his line-end sounds? Why? Would you prefer this poem without so many sound repetitions? Why or why not?

4. In the following poem which of the words in brackets would be more suitable because of their sounds? (In several cases the choice is arguable.)

BEARS

Wonderful / Marvellous / Mysterious
bears that walked my room {all / at / by} night,

Where are you gone, {your / with / that} sleek and {silky / magic / fairy} fur,

Your eyes' veiled imperious light?

<table><tr><td rowspan="3">Brown bears as rich as {</td><td>mocha</td><td rowspan="3">or as musk,</td></tr><tr><td>coffee</td></tr><tr><td>chocolate</td></tr></table>

<table><tr><td rowspan="3">White {</td><td>rainbow tinted</td><td rowspan="3">bears whose fur stood out</td></tr><tr><td>glittering</td></tr><tr><td>opalescent</td></tr></table>

<table><tr><td rowspan="3">Electric in the {</td><td>glowing</td><td rowspan="3">dusk,</td></tr><tr><td>creeping</td></tr><tr><td>deepening</td></tr></table>

<table><tr><td rowspan="3">And {</td><td>huge</td><td></td></tr><tr><td>great</td><td>black bears who seemed more blue than black</td></tr><tr><td>thick</td><td></td></tr></table>

<table><tr><td rowspan="3">More {</td><td>violet</td><td rowspan="3">than blue against the dark —</td></tr><tr><td>navy blue</td></tr><tr><td>midnight blue</td></tr></table>

Where are you now? Upon what track

<table><tr><td rowspan="3">Mutter your {</td><td>padded</td><td rowspan="3">paws, that used to tread</td></tr><tr><td>muffled</td></tr><tr><td>stealthy</td></tr></table>

<table><tr><td rowspan="3">So softly, surely up the {</td><td>unsqueaking</td><td rowspan="3">stair</td></tr><tr><td>silent</td></tr><tr><td>creakless</td></tr></table>

<table><tr><td rowspan="3">While I lay {</td><td>trembling</td><td rowspan="3">in bed?</td></tr><tr><td>listening</td></tr><tr><td>shivering</td></tr></table>

<table><tr><td rowspan="3">When did I {</td><td>drop</td><td rowspan="3">you? Whose have you become?</td></tr><tr><td>leave</td></tr><tr><td>lose</td></tr></table>

<table><tr><td rowspan="3">Why do I wait and {</td><td>wait</td><td rowspan="3">and never hear</td></tr><tr><td>fear</td></tr><tr><td>hark</td></tr></table>

<table><tr><td rowspan="3">Your thick {</td><td>nightly</td><td rowspan="3">pacing in my room?</td></tr><tr><td>nocturnal</td></tr><tr><td>evening</td></tr></table>

My bears, who { keeps / bears / hears } you now, in pride and fear?

ADRIENNE RICH

5. Listen to someone taking a shower or washing dishes or a car. Or listen to a playground, a street at midnight or noon, a library, bus, cafeteria, or department store, a woods at dawn, noon, or sunset. Or listen to silence. Make a list of everything you hear at that time and place in as minute detail as words will let you, at least two pages' worth. Select from your list the twelve to fifteen items that most clearly recreate your mood in that place at that time. Select and sequence to emphasize that mood. Give your poem a title. Then ask the class to suggest changes of rhythm or sound that would help support your title.
6. Take a word for a sensation other than hearing, such as *soft, thick, sharp*, or *blue, red, brown, black*, and answer the question, "What does *sharp* or *blue*, etc. sound like? Free associate for two pages or ten minutes, then examine your raw material for traces of a felt idea, and select and sequence to see whether rhythm and sound can be further modified to support your felt idea.
7. Write a curse or lullaby or quarrel entirely in nonsense syllables, as if you heard it at a distance and could distinguish only the rhythm and sounds. Next replace your nonsense syllables with words of appropriate meaning, with as nearly as possible the same rhythms and sounds. Ask the class to title it. If you disagree, ask their help in revising toward your own title.

MULTIPLE CONNOTATIONS

Which of the following does the word *green* suggest to you?

> *slime, buds, satin, mint, leaves, warm air, rotten meat, grass, snake, new shoes, toothpaste, pea soup, dollar bills, mailboxes, stagnant pools, wormy cheese, glass beads, grass-stained knees, dragon fly, May fly*

If you select *slime, snake, rotten meat, stagnant pools*, and *wormy cheese*, green suggests decay to you. If you select *buds, mint, leaves*, and *warm air*, green suggests growing life, spring. If you select *toothpaste, pea soup, mailboxes, dollar bills*, and *grass-stained knees*, it reminds you of a comfortable suburban domestic life. If you select *warm air, glass beads, new shoes*, and *satin*, it suggests romance. But suppose you choose *satin, glass beads, new shoes, mint* and *snake*? You create a surprise, almost a shock, like a serpent in Eden. Or suppose you take *warm air, rotten meat; new shoes, stained knees; May fly, stagnant pool*? You have chosen contrasts that sound a note of warning.

Such differences of meaning? When everyone knows what the word *green* objectively and scientifically means? The dictionary says that *green* is "any color between blue and yellow in the spectrum." It can be "produced by blending blue and yellow pigments." No feeling in that definition. No hope for growth or fear of decay. Your own varied reactions to the word illustrate the way that a single objective meaning (*denotation*) acquires multiple emotional meanings (*connotations*). Words are used over and over again in situations that cause emotions. After enough repetition, anything associated with an event, including any word, will cause the same emotional reaction as the whole situation originally did. Many words, especially common ones like colors, have been used in so many contradictory situations that they provoke contradictory connotations. For example, *cat* connotes, to some people, softness of fur, contented sound of purring, the alertness of pointed ears, the cleanness of a carefully licked paw. To others it connotes the stealth of stalking a prey, the sharpness of claws, the ear-splitting yowl at midnight, the dead bird on the doorstep. *Blanket* connotes warmth, softness, security; it also connotes smothering, smog, overprotection. *Cave* connotes safety, shelter, a cozy hideout; it also connotes damp, dark, bats, and bones. If you use these words with regard only for their denotations, you may give your reader the right *idea*, but the wrong *feeling* or a confusing conflict of feelings. If you use them in awareness of their connotations, you may be able to use multiple feelings to create a unified idea.

7 multiple meanings

THE SPOON

An old spoon
Bent, gouged,
Polished to an evil
Glitter.

It has bitten
Into my life —
This kennel-bone
Sucked thin.

Now it is a living
Thing: ready
To scratch a name
On a prison wall —

Ready to be passed on
To the little one
Just barely
Beginning to walk.

CHARLES SIMIC

The denotation of *spoon* is "a utensil consisting of a small, shallow, usually oval-shaped bowl and a handle, used in eating and cooking for picking up or stirring food or drink." It has been used in wealth and poverty, for food or medicine, in babyhood and senility, by one's own hand and by the hand of a mother or nurse or jailor. But its most common connotation is that of comfortable, common usefulness. Simic has drawn on its more sinister connotations — a worn spoon, worn not only with use, but with abuse, worn thin and therefore sharp, sharp enough to scratch back, and ready for the next generation to use as a weapon. Kinds of use can make any tool into both a promise and a threat. Simic could not have surprised us into that awareness so quickly and so intensely if he had not noticed that the word *spoon* has two kinds of connotations and moved us from one to the other.

EXERCISES

1. Which of the following words for the same things have pleasant connotations, unpleasant, both, neither?

   Bread, money, green stuff, dough, finances, wherewithal.
   Scold, bawl out, reprimand, castigate, correct, reprove.
   Home, pad, house, domicile, living quarters, residence.

2. Among the following words with pleasant connotations, how many kinds of pleasantness can you distinguish?

   Good, delicious, delightful, pleasant, yummy, exquisite, charming, sweet, tough, OK, wonderful, nice, tops, admirable, pretty good, super, fine, excellent, darling, superior, superb, lovely, divine.

3. In the following poem how would the following substitutions affect the felt idea? Would you advise the poet to make any of them? Which? Why?

TRUTH

For me a shimmer a quiver on skin or linen
an opal set in a toad's face

I squeeze whatever squeezes and may be food
I peel whatever sticks

A white eye is an oiled hand is an apron
is a bell

And you who are right and know it
square your chin at me through milk

Substitutions: for *quiver: ripple, wavelet, shiver*; for *toad's: snake's, skunk's, pig's*; for *food: drink, sweet, tasty*; for *sticks: stays, waits, remains*; for *apron: blanket, sandal, raincoat*; for *bell: shell, veil, cane*; for *milk: mist, silk, fog.*

4. Take the items you chose from the list of things associated with *green.* Free associate about half a page more that suggest the same kind of greenness. Select the half dozen of these associations that go best with the ones you already have. Make them into a poem. Ask the class to suggest a title. Have they perceived the felt idea you thought you had put there? If not, did they find a better one? A conflicting one? None at all? Revise toward what you now think you want to say.
5. Do the same as in No. 4 for one of the following words: *grease, wet, soft, gold, white, high.* In revising toward a poem, consider not only matters of connotation, but also structure, rhythm, and sound.

MULTIPLE DENOTATIONS

If you leaf through the dictionary, you will find that most words have not only one denotation, with several connotations, but several denotations, each with its own connotations. Take, for example, the word *cross.* Free associate on that word for the usual two pages or ten minutes. How many separate denotations do you find? Now consult your college dictionary. How many more do you find? The college edition of Webster's *New World Dictionary* (1970) lists 13 denotations for *sing*, 26 for *wear*, 34 for *right*, 19 for *green*, and 20 for *white.* You could use any one of these words unambiguously in any one of its denotations. Straight information has to do so. There is no ambiguity in saying, "She won't be crossed," "The teacher crossed out my answer," "Be careful not to cross her path," or "Cross the witch's palm with silver, and you may be safe."

But what about (1) "The graveyard cross corrects her fatal error" or (2) "Cross her path, cross her palm;/but cross her will, cross out your own" or (3) "On her white breast a sparkling cross she wore/which Jews might kiss and infidels adore"? In the first example, the grave marker and the teacher's correction mark are fused to emphasize that some mistakes are trivial and easily corrected, but that others are corrected only by death. In the second, four denotations of *cross* are used together to warn that some evil (she) can be bribed, but not defied. And in the third, *cross* is used to mean both religious symbol and jewelry, to satirize the frivolous life style of a society girl.

EXERCISES

1. In the following poem what two denotations of the word *struck* does the poet use in the last line? How are they both simultaneously true?

EIGHT O'CLOCK

He stood, and heard the steeple
  Sprinkle the quarters on the morning town.
One, two, three, four, to market-place and people
  It tossed them down.

Strapped, noosed, nighing his hour,
  He stood and counted them and cursed his luck;
And then the clock collected in the tower
  Its strength, and struck.

A. E. HOUSMAN

2. What are the multiple meanings in each of the following poems?

HISTORY OF IDEAS

God is love. Then by conversion
Love is God, and sex conversion.

J. V. CUNNINGHAM

WHEN I SHALL BE WITHOUT REGRET

When I shall be without regret
And shall mortality forget,
When I shall die who lived for this,
I shall not miss the things I miss.
And you who notice where I lie
Ask not my name. It is not I.

J. V. CUNNINGHAM

3. What denotations does the word *changes* have in the following poem? Why do you think the poet used it in more than one meaning?

THE BEAUTIFUL CHANGES

One wading a Fall meadow finds on all sides
The Queen Anne's Lace lying like lilies
On water; it glides
So from the walker, it turns
Dry grass to a lake, as the slightest shade of you
Valleys my mind in fabulous blue Lucernes.

The beautiful changes as a forest is changed
By a chameleon's tuning his skin to it;
As a mantis, arranged
On a green leaf, grows
Into it, makes the leaf leafier, and proves
Any greenness is deeper than anyone knows.

Your hands hold roses always in a way that says
They are not only yours; the beautiful changes
In such kind ways,
Wishing ever to sunder
Things and things' selves for a second finding, to lose
For a moment all that it touches back to wonder.

RICHARD WILBUR

4. Think of something about which you have strong but simultaneously mixed feelings: a relative, an animal, a place, getting up at sunrise, running, shovelling snow, etc. Free associate the usual two pages or ten minutes. Select and sequence the ten to fifteen items that most strongly express your mixture of feelings. Again by the strategy of asking the class to give your poem a title, discover whether you have said what you thought and hoped you said.
5. Cruise through the dictionary, preferably the *Oxford English Dictionary*, certainly nothing smaller than a college dictionary, and select a common word with a long entry, such as *need, die, marry, give, arch, pity, loss.* Take down meanings that attract your attention and quotations illustrating those that seem interesting. Return to your list later. Select and sequence to emphasize the contradictions in the word, both connotative and denotative. Ask your class how many contradictions they can find in your list. Develop into a poem.

CONTEXTS

Suppose you are a tourist exploring the partly uncovered ruins of an ancient city state. You stop before the remains of a colossal statue of an emperor. All that's left are two huge stone legs, and on the ground part of a face. The pedestal says, "My name is Ozymandias, King of Kings:/ Look on my works, ye Mighty, and despair!" What Ozymandias thought he said *then* and what he says *now* are exactly opposite, because the surroundings (*context*) have changed. You, whom he meant to despair because you could not build a city as mighty as the city spread out before the statue, now despair because there is no city. You conclude that no one can make anything that really lasts.

OZYMANDIAS

I met a traveler from an antique land
Who said: Two vast and trunkless legs of stone
Stand in the desert. . . . Near them, on the sand,
Half sunk, a shattered visage lies, whose frown,
And wrinkled lip, and sneer of cold command,
Tell that its sculptor well those passions read
Which yet survive, stamped on these lifeless things,

The hand that mocked them, and the heart that fed:
And on the pedestal these words appear:
"My name is Ozymandias, King of Kings:
Look on my works, ye Mighty, and despair!"
Nothing beside remains. Round the decay
Of that colossal wreck, boundless and bare
The lone and level sands stretch far away.

PERCY BYSSHE SHELLEY

Context works in the same way in Ben Jonson's "On My First Son":

ON MY FIRST SON

Farewell, thou child of my right hand,[1] and joy;
My sin was too much hope of thee, loved boy:
Seven years thou'wert lent to me, and I thee pay,
Exacted by thy fate, on the just day.[2]
O could I lose all father now! for why
Will man lament the state he should envý,
To have so soon 'scaped world's and flesh's rage,
And, if no other misery, yet age?
Rest in soft peace, and asked, say, "Here doth lie
Ben Jonson his best piece of poetry."
For whose sake henceforth all his vows be such
As what he loves may never like too much.

The word *like* is normally used as a pale version of *love*: "I like you, John, but I don't love you enough to marry you," "I like the dress (picture, house, food, town), but I don't love it." But Jonson's context has made the word *like* into a richer, more intimate *love*. A man will love his son just because it is a convention, almost a duty to love one's own child. But liking is a matter of choice. It suggests relaxed enjoyment and companionship. To enjoy a duty is rare. To both love and like a son is an unusually strong caring.

[1]The child's name, *Benjamin,* literally means "child of my right hand."
[2]The child died on his seventh birthday.

The following poem is apparently written to mourn the death of a child:

BELLS FOR JOHN WHITESIDE'S DAUGHTER

There was such speed in her little body,
And such lightness in her footfall,
It is no wonder her brown study
Astonishes us all.

Her wars were bruited in our high window.
We looked among orchard trees and beyond
Where she took arms against her shadow,
Or harried unto the pond

The lazy geese, like a snow cloud
Dripping their snow on the green grass,
Tricking and stopping, sleepy and proud,
Who cried in goose, Alas,

For the tireless heart within the little
Lady with rod that made them rise
From their noon apple-dreams and scuttle
Goose-fashion under the skies!

But now go the bells, and we are ready,
In one house we are sternly stopped
To say we are vexed at her brown study,
Lying so primly propped.

JOHN CROWE RANSOM

Astonishes, in line 4, and *vexed*, in line 19, are not the usual words to express grief. *Brown study*[3], line 3, and *primly propped*, line 20, are not the usual phrases to describe a dead body laid out in a funeral home to be viewed by friends and relatives. The poet has made us more aware of the

[3] One is said to be *in a brown study* when one is concentrating so hard on some inner thought that one does not notice what is going on around one and does not respond when spoken to.

meaning of death by denying us the words that usually comfort the living on such occasions: *sweet child, flower, innocent, too young to die, her mother's comfort and her father's joy.* This use of words out of their usual context has denied us the comfort of the usual sticky sentiment that we cover death with to make it acceptable, and made us face its full cruelty. The poet wants to make us really angry and profoundly sad.

Another way that context multiples meaning is by *allusion* or *reference* to a bit of history or literature familiar enough so that just a word or two will flash the whole experience past the reader. Poets use *names* (Mary, Eve, Venus, Helen, Job, Lincoln, Bluebeard, Rapunzel, Daniel Boone, Martin Luther King); *places* (Eden, Washington, Atlantis, Shangri La, Everest); *forms* (recipes, questionnaires, want ads, menus, proverbs, epitaphs, political speeches); *cliché phrases* (pleased to meet you, out of the ordinary, sincerely yours, long time no see, touch ground) — anything that will remind readers of facts, people, attitudes, actions and their meanings that are already a part of their common experience. Poets also use these bits of history and familiar forms and phrases to set up expectations and then disappoint them in order to say something different of their own.

For example, the following poem is in the form of the Ten Commandments:

THE LATEST DECALOGUE

Thou shalt have one God only; who
Would be at the expense of two?
No graven images may be
Worshipped, except the currency.
Swear not at all; for, for they curse
Thine enemy is none the worse.
At church on Sunday to attend
Will serve to keep the world thy friend.
Honor thy parents; that is, all
From whom advancement may befall.
Thou shalt not kill; but need'st not strive
Officiously to keep alive.
Do not adultery commit;
Advantage rarely comes of it.
Thou shalt not steal; an empty feat,
When it's so lucrative to cheat.

Bear not false witness; let the lie
Have time on its own wings to fly.
Thou shalt not covet; but tradition
Approves all forms of competition.

ARTHUR HUGH CLOUGH

Although this poem is in the form of the Ten Commandments, they are not like the commandments Moses received on Mt. Sinai. These are directions to worldly people for worldly success. The point seems to be to make merely "practical" believers feel ashamed. The poet has rebuffed the reader's expectation in order to create satire.

The following poem is in another familiar form, a newspaper report from a battlefront:

THE PERSIAN VERSION

Truth-loving Persians do not dwell upon
The trivial skirmish fought near Marathon.[4]
As for the Greek theatrical tradition
Which represents that summer's expedition
Not as a mere reconnaissance in force
By three brigades of foot and one of horse
(Their left flank covered by some obsolete
Light craft detached from the main Persian fleet)
But as a grandiose, ill-starred attempt
To conquer Greece — they treat it with contempt;
And only incidentally refute
Major Greek claims, by stressing what repute
The Persian monarch and the Persian nation
Won by this salutary demonstration:
Despite a strong defense and adverse weather
All arms combined magnificently together.

ROBERT GRAVES

Is this poem really about the Battle of Marathon? Why didn't Graves use a contemporary military engagement? What, in your opinion, is he satirizing?

[4] The Athenian version is that at the Battle of Marathon, 490 B.C., the Athenians killed 6400 Persians and lost only 192 of their own men and that although the Athenians were badly outnumbered, the Persians had to be rescued by their fleet.

The following poem looks like the kind of brief questionnaire about beliefs called a catechism:

SOME LAST QUESTIONS

What is the head
A. Ash
What are the eyes
A. The wells have fallen in and have
Inhabitants
What are the feet
A. Thumbs left after the auction
No what are the feet
A. Under them the impossible road is moving
Down which the broken necked mice push
Balls of blood with their noses
What is the tongue
A. The black coat that fell off the wall
With sleeves trying to say something
What are the hands
A. Paid
No what are the hands
A. Climbing back down the museum wall
To their ancestors the extinct shrews that will
Have left a message
What is the silence
A. As though it had a right to more
Who are the compatriots
A. They make the stars of bone

W. S. Merwin

In catechisms both questions and answers are formulas to be memorized. But Merwin has used the form to ask questions whose answers can't be memorized, because they are *last* questions and can be answered only after death. What do the *hands, eyes, feet*, and *tongue* mean outside their normal physical and social contexts? What is the *silence* (meaning, nature) of the universe outside our living perceptions of it? Who are our compatriots then? In this situation the wrong answers are the pat, worldly answers that the *hands* are *paid* and that the *feet* are the useless remains after the *auction* (the business of living) is over. The answers he accepts describe a gradual disintegration of consciousness from human to animal to mineral. Where a religious catechism would give assurances of afterlife, Merwin's gives only assurances of extinction. To promise mortality in a form that usually promises immortality gives us a nasty shock.

EXERCISES

1. Identify the kinds of allusion in the following poems in Poems for Further Discussion and explain why the poets used them: W. H. Auden, "The Unknown Citizen"; cummings, "next to of course god america i"; Kennedy, "Epitaph for a Postal Clerk"; Yeats, "Leda and the Swan."
2. As fast as you can, write two pages or more of nonsense in one of the following forms: recipes, proverbs, want ads, menus, postal addresses, sandwiches, or any other familiar form your instructor agrees to. Let it cool an hour or a day. Come back and see if your "nonsense" has suggested any pattern that might be the felt idea of a poem. Select, sequence, and complete, using all the skills of structure, rhythm, sound, and multiple meaning you have practiced thus far. Ask your class to title it. If their titles indicate that the felt idea has not come through, ask them to help revise it in your direction — or change directions.

Good poems can be made without much, if any, multiple meaning, but even the quietest, most understated poets tend to use some, if only because concreteness itself brings conflicting associations; and many twentieth-century poets use as much as they can. To conclude the chapter, let us examine a poem that uses several kinds together:

DESIGN

I found a dimpled spider, fat and white,
On a white heal-all, holding up a moth
Like a white piece of rigid satin cloth —
Assorted characters of death and blight
Mixed ready to begin the morning right,
Like the ingredients of a witches' broth —
A snow-drop spider, a flower like froth,
And dead wings carried like a paper kite.

What had that flower to do with being white,
The wayside blue and innocent heal-all?
What brought the kindred spider to that height,
Then steered the white moth thither in the night?
What but design of darkness to appall? —
If design govern in a thing so small.

ROBERT FROST

Frost's overall purpose is to shock his reader and himself into realizing freshly that we live in a hostile, perhaps deliberately hostile, universe. His technique is to set up expectations and then reward them with something else. The sonnet form makes us expect a statement, a logical progression toward a firm conclusion, but this sonnet ends on an apparent afterthought. He uses the word *white* five times in a context that leaves no doubt that he is setting the connotations of purity, cleanliness, and innocence associated with white satin, dimpled plumpness, and snow against the connotations of sickliness, deformity, and death: a *heal-all* is normally a blue flower; a spider large enough to carry a moth is most often brown or black; and a moth is usually brown or spotted. The word *design* denotes either a pattern or a threatening plot. The word *small* means both something small in size, as this scene actually is, or unimportant. *Darkness* means not only a literal night, but the principle of evil. If darkness designs to appall, it must have evil intent.

EXERCISES

1. How have the poets of the following poems (see Poems for Further Discussion) created multiple meaning by disappointing a reader's expectation of denotation, connotation, or context? How has this disappointment contributed to each poet's meaning? Blake, "The Tiger"; Justice, "Counting the Mad"; Eliot, "Sweeney Among the Nightingales"; Bogan, "The Crossed Apple"; Dickinson, "A Narrow Fellow in the Grass"; Kennedy, "Ars Poetica"; Frost, "Range-Finding."
2. Answer the following questionnaire three times. Say something different each time, moving from factual truth to wishful lies to the wildest impossibilities. Read over the three sets of answers and select those that surprise and interest you most. Select and sequence into a poem.

Questionnaire:
Who are you?
How many fingers, how many hands?
Are you tall enough to ___ low enough to ___?
Where are you now? Where were you then?
What have you said that you'd rather not say? That you'd say again?
What do you eat? Whom do you eat?
Where will you go? What will you bring?
Have you other names?
Have you a ring? What kind of ring?
What's on your feet?
The name of your street?
Anywhere special you'd rather not wait?
Where do you hurt?
Where do you hunt?
How high can you climb?
How far could you swim, at night, in the rain?

3. Try to find a standard intelligence test. Answer it by picking out all the most wrong answers. Select about a dozen you wish were true. Make those into a poem.

Have you ever been angry with *Mother Nature*? Been *catty* to your neighbor? *Eaten crow*? Literally, no. Nature is not a person, much less a mother. You cannot twitch your tail, draw back your fingernails, and purr. And as for crow, even if the supermarket had crow, you couldn't bear to eat it. Yet in another sense, yes. You've probably been and done all these things. To *eat crow* would be to apologize against your will; to be *catty* would be to make unkind remarks behind a person's back; and to be angry with Mother Nature would be to be irritated by inconsistent or unpleasant weather. The process of finding likenesses in things that are basically unlike is called *metaphor*. A word that has no concreteness of its own is given concreteness by being likened to some *thing* that shares one or more of its intangible qualities. *Eat crow* and *apologize* share only your unwillingness to do them. *Catty* and *sneakily cruel* share only the quality of unexpected hurt. *Rain-sun-wind* and *mother* share only their sometimes harsh, sometimes kind control. The word that needs concreteness in order to be more fully understood is called the *tenor*; the thing it borrows size, shape, sound, and texture from is called the *vehicle*. *Mother Nature* is the vehicle for *natural forces; catty* is the vehicle for *sneakily cruel; eat crow* is the vehicle for *apologize*.

Metaphor is not the same as a comparison between things that are really alike. "She is like her sister" or "Despair is like depression" are literally true. The concreteness or lack of it is the same in both words compared. The purpose is not to explain one in terms of another that is mostly different, but to show how the two are mostly the same. *Comparison* is a close *look; metaphor* is a *leap*. Metaphor tells the truth by telling lies.

Consider what lie tells what truth in each of the following:

Life is a bowl of cherries.

Happiness is a warm puppy.

Justice is a blindfolded goddess holding a scales.

Power is a big stick.

Each of these tenors (*life, happiness, justice, power*) is abstracted from so many and such complex experiences that suggesting all of them would be impossible. Even listing them would require more abstractions. *Life* would have to be divided into *pain, joy, fear, poverty, sickness, success*, just to begin. *Justice* would be *inflexibility* and *incompetence* as well as *fairness*. But fortunately the full range of meanings is not usually wanted all at once. Here all the speaker wants us to know is that life is good and bad; that happi-

8 metaphor

ness is physical comfort, affection, and companionship; that justice is impartial; and that power is physical force. The cherries, puppy, blindfolded goddess, and big stick convey these denotations instantly and reinforce them with connotations.

EXERCISES

1. What sort of person does the following poem describe? What is the poet's attitude toward Chloe? How does each vehicle the poet has chosen clarify the tenor of Chloe's character? The tenor of the poet's attitude?

LOVE SONG

for Chloe

I guess your beauty doesn't
bother you, you wear it easy
and walk across the driveway
so casual and right it makes

my heart weigh twenty pounds
as I back out and wave
thinking She's my summer
peaches, corn, long moondawn dusks
watermelons chilling in a tub
of ice and water: mirrored there
the great midsummer sky
rolling with clouds and treetops
and down by the lake
the wild canaries
swinging on the horse mint
all morning long.

DAVID YOUNG

2. What personality traits might the following be vehicles for: an *axe*, a *porcupine*, an *eel*, a *sow on ice*, a *vine*, a *wind*, a *blank page*, a *well*, a *rock*, a *hen with one chick*? Pick one of these that fits a person you know. Free associate a page of other things that would also fit that person. Decide what attitude toward the person your list shows. Select and sequence into a poem.
3. Pick an abstraction, such as *courage, shame, envy, caring, greed, hope, worship, curiosity, bless, blame*, that you feel especially familiar with. Put the word at the top of the page. Then free associate a couple of pages of things. Do *not* check them as you go along to see whether they illustrate the word at the top of the page. Exchange lists with other members of the class and ask them to choose the dozen or so things from your list that somehow suit the word. Do you agree? Which would you add or remove from their selection to embody your own idea of the word's meaning? Edit your revised selection into a poem.

VARIETIES OF METAPHOR

The following statements say the same thing, in a sequence from literal to metaphorical:

1. Dead deep-rooted vegetation indicated the proximity of desert.
2. A dead tree marked the edge of the desert.

3. As clearly as a signpost, a dead tree marked the edge of the desert.
4. A dead tree was the signpost marking the edge of the desert.
5. A dead tree beckoned and pointed to the edge of the desert.
6. The guide stopped and pointed to a dead tree.

Statement 1 is a literal, nonmetaphorical general and abstract statement. Statement 2 is also literal, but specific and concrete. *Deep-rooted vegetation* has become *tree, proximity* has become *edge*, and a specific desert place is indicated by *the*. Statement 3 is metaphor, in the form called *simile* (tenor and vehicle joined by *like* or *as*). The tree is not literally a signpost, but it shares with road signs and street signs the function of pointing to what is beyond it. Statement 4 is the same signpost simile in different syntax. The word indicating comparison, *as*, has been omitted and the words *tree* and *signpost* have been joined by *is*. Saying that the tenor *is* the vehicle is called *metaphor*, in the narrow sense of the word. Statement 5 gives human qualities to the tree (*personification*). It is actively signalling what is ahead as if it had arms and fingers. Statement 6 is the literal tree again, but in a context in which a reader will see it as a sign, a warning, and a prophecy of approaching desert and so of approaching death for anything or anyone that risks the circumstances that killed it. Used in that context often enough, the dead tree will become that form of metaphor known as *symbol*. A book entitled *The Dead Tree* would suggest the gradual starvation and death of a relationship or an institution or a creative talent, without needing to be explained.

Metaphor comes in additional specialized forms with their own names:

1. Very long and complex comparisons of things radically unlike (*conceit*: see Marvell's "On a Drop of Dew," p. 170, and Campion's "There Is a Garden in Her Face," p. 145).
2. A story in which each place, character, and action is metaphorical and the whole story stands for a moral, political, or religious idea (*allegory*: see Wilbur's "Shame," p. 101, and Merwin's "The Egg," p. 171.
3. A comparison between a pair of relationships (*analogy*: a:b::c:d. She loves clothes the way Winnie the Pooh loves honey.)
4. Apparent nonsense that can have no relevant literal meaning in its context and, therefore, if it means anything at all, must mean something else and so sets the reader searching (*surrealism*: see Benedikt's "Divine Love," p. 36, and Péret's "Hello," p. 106.

There are also metaphors that are no longer metaphors and are no longer meant to be: a *square meal*, the *goal of the course, plain truth, sound investment, firm resolve, deep thinking, foundation of the faith.* These must once have had metaphorical force. Gold coins, for instance, were once square; people would file off bits to make more coins, so that a rounded corner on a coin came to mean less than your money's worth, and a square coin — or meal — would have full value. A *course* is literally a race toward a goal post, but who remembers this while sitting in class jotting down the causes of the French Revolution or summarizing them on an exam? *Sound* originally meant healthy, to be tested by stethoscope and the doctor's thumping. Stock shares and compound interest can't be thumped. All these are called *dead metaphors.* Their long use in the same contexts has first made them clichés, acceptable for everyday and business communication, but incapable of conveying any fresh awareness; still longer use in the same contexts has leached out all their metaphorical meaning and finally killed them.

Suppose someone dear to you said, "Darling, do you love me?" And suppose you answered:

Darling, do I love you?
Foundation of my being,
Profound depths of my feeling,
My goal is to show you,
My firm resolve to prove
The plain truth of my love.

This poem might well strike your loved one as insincere, because the metaphors are so stale that the reader would miss the heaving of brick and mortar, in the second line, the straining to reach an arm down farther than it can go, in the third line, the aching legs, in the fourth, the tightening muscles all over the body, in the fifth, and the picture of a loved gesture or mouth in the last line. *Cliché* (trite, stale) metaphors are always dying. If they are recognized as metaphors at all, they have lost their power to surprise and will cause only the "So what" or the "Oh, that again" reaction from alert readers — unless the poet changes a cliché's wording or context just enough so that readers recognize it as they would any other allusion and are surprised by its new meaning. Notice how William Stafford brings to life the cliché *blind faith* in "How It Began," p. 184; how Wallace Stevens revives the cliché *new fangled* in "Of Mere Being," p. 184; and how Michael Benedikt gives new life to the overquoted "Of the people, by the people, for the people" in "The Moralist of Bananas," p. 142.

WAYS OF USING METAPHOR

This compulsion to find *abstract meanings* in *things* and *likenesses* in *unlikes*, this habit of metaphor, so dominates our seeing and our language that poets could not avoid it if they chose. Some choose, however, to match tenor with vehicle, often in great detail; whereas, some describe a vehicle in detail and leave the reader to guess the tenor. Consider the following poems, each of which consists of a single metaphor:

1. SHAME

It is a cramped little state with no foreign policy,
Save to be thought inoffensive. The grammar of the language
Has never been fathomed, owing to the national habit
Of allowing each sentence to trail off in confusion.
Those who have visited Scusi, the capital city,
Report that the railway-route from Schuldig passes
Through country best described as unrelieved.
Sheep are the national product. The faint inscription
Over the city gates may perhaps be rendered,
"I'm afraid you won't find much of interest here."
Census-reports which give the population
As zero are, of course, not to be trusted,
Save as reflecting the natives' flustered insistence
That they do not count, as well as their modest horror
Of letting one's sex be known in so many words.
The uniform grey of the nondescript buildings, the absence
Of churches or comfort-stations, have given observers
An odd impression of ostentatious meanness,
And it must be said of the citizens (muttering by
In their ratty sheepskins, shying at cracks in the sidewalk)
That they lack the peace of mind of the truly humble.
The tenor of life is careful, even in the stiff
Unsmiling carelessness of the border-guards
And *douaniers*, who admit, whenever they can,
Not merely the usual carloads of deodorant
But gypsies, g-strings, hasheesh, and contraband pigments.
Their complete negligence is reserved, however,
For the hoped-for invasion, at which time the happy people

(Sniggering, ruddily naked, and shamelessly drunk)
Will stun the foe by their overwhelming submission,
Corrupt the generals, infiltrate the staff,
Usurp the throne, proclaim themselves to be sun-gods,
And bring about the collapse of the whole empire.

RICHARD WILBUR

Shame (the tenor) is equated with a *state* or *nation* (the vehicle). That, of course, is literally impossible, but a state or nation is composed of people, and people have shame. Shame makes people self-effacing and unwilling to say anything definite, which in a state would take the form of no foreign policy, a language with no complete sentences, a capital whose name translates as "Excuse Me," a landscape without prominent features, a census that lets nobody count or be counted, and buildings that all look alike. Sheep are a common metaphor for meek, docile ashamed people. The first sixteen lines show the cringing quality of shame. But there's a boastful, aggressive quality about shame too. The lack of churches and public toilets, the ratty sheepskins the people wear, their shying at sidewalk cracks, the careful carelessness of the border-guards, their willingness to import both respectable trivia and dangerous amounts of sex and drugs into the country — all seem to show a self-conscious, self-congratulating, calculating kind of humbleness that's not humble at all, a sort of "congratulate-me-I'm-humbler-than-thou" attitude that is a reverse pride. That kind of pride will cause such total submission to an enemy, such extremely shameful acts, such shameful contamination of others that the conqueror, who was originally unashamed, will become as shameful as those he thought he'd conquered. Wilbur is saying, "Shame is not an honest humbleness but a strategy for power." This poem extends metaphor as far as allegory.

2. TO PAINT THE PORTRAIT OF A BIRD

For Elsa Henriquez

First of all paint a cage
its door standing open
then paint
something appealing
something shining

something beautiful
something tasty
for the bird
then lean the canvas up against a tree
in a garden
in a forest
or in the woods
find another tree and hide yourself behind it
silently
without moving a muscle...
Sometimes the bird will come right away
but it could also take many long years
before it decides to
Don't become discouraged
but wait
wait if you have to year after year after year
the earliness or lateness of its arrival
has no relation
to the success of the work
When the bird appears
if he appears
maintain the most total silence
while you wait for the bird to enter the cage
and once he's in
softly shut the door with a quick stroke of your paintbrush
then
one by one blot out all the bars of the cage
taking care not to touch the bird's feathers
Then paint the tree's portrait
choosing the most beautiful of all its branches
for the bird
also paint the green foliage and the freshness of the breeze
the dust afloat in the sunlight
and the noises of the insects in the grass in the intense heat of
summer
and then wait for the bird to sing
If the bird does not sing
it's a bad sign
a sign that the picture is bad
but if it does sing that's a good sign
that is to say a sign that you can sign

Then you reach out and gently pluck
one of the feathers of the bird
and you write your name over in one corner of the picture.

JACQUES PRÉVERT
Translated by Michael Benedikt

In "To Paint a Portrait of a Bird" we are given no tenor, and the vehicle is a literally impossible event: a man tries to catch a bird by painting a picture of a cage, with its pictured door open and a pictured bait inside. He hides and waits, moments or years, until a bird comes and enters the painted cage. Then he paints the cage door shut. Next he paints a suitable setting for the bird: a tree, fresh breeze, dust motes in sunlight, heat of summer, and noise of insects. If the bird likes it and sings, the artist can sign his name to the picture with one of its feathers. The literal impossibility of a real bird caught in a painting of a cage forces the reader to look for what it stands for. What part of a work of art causes it to start, causes it to take perhaps years, causes the kind and extent of changes the artist will make as it develops, and determines whether it works (comes alive) at the end? Perhaps some controlling force *invited* but not *created* by the artist? For *bird* you might substitute that *felt idea* from the subconscious mind that you have been inviting in every writing exercise in this book.

3. THE FIRST PLANET AFTER HER DEATH

A dog lopes across a meadow
taking a lot of time to get there,
wherever it thinks it is going.
It is not going anywhere, this dog

(watching it from a great way
to one side, one side of what?
one side of the field, watching
its hind legs coming down each time
a little to the left of the front,
tracking a little to one side)

this dog taking a very long time
to make it over, the whole field,
sometimes loping through grass
almost tall enough to hide him

then being gone from the field,
the sun going down, the stars
crossing overhead and being gone
in turn, crossing the grass field.

RICHARD SOMMER

"The First Planet After Her Death" is an example of accurate literal details selected and sequenced to imply metaphor. It describes a dog loping across a field and disappearing, then the sun, then the stars. There is nothing in the poem which *must* be taken as metaphor in order to be understood. Even the title can be read as literally true. It could be literally the first time that the poet has looked at the planet Earth after the death of someone close to him. Still, it is an unusual title. Sommer could so easily have called it "The First Summer After Her Death" or "The First Walk in the Fields Without Her." The title makes us wonder if the poem is going to say something about the cosmology of death. This suspicion is strengthened by the order of the events described in the poem: day disappears, then sun, then stars. At this point certain apparently random remarks about the dog take on additional meaning: the fact that the direction of its hind legs is slightly different from the direction of its front legs; the fact that it thinks it's going somewhere but is not; the fact, repeated, that it takes a long time to cross the field; the fact that the grass sometimes hides it; the repetition of *gone* for the dog's and the stars' disappearance and the repetition of *across, crossing* and *crossing* for dog, sun, and stars. The dog's journey across the field suggests the journey of life, but the work of providing that meaning has been left almost entirely to the reader.

4. HELLO

My airplane in flames my Rhinewine-flooded castle
my ghetto of black iris my crystal ear
my rock slipping off a cliff to crush the local police-chief
my opal snail my mosquito made out of air
my bird-of-paradise mattress my hair of black foam
my exploded grave my rain of red grasshoppers
my flying island my turquoise grape
my collision of wise and foolish autos my wild flower bed
my dandelion pistil stuck in my eye
my tulip bulb in the brain
my gazelle wandering through a moviehouse at midnight in the
    midtown area
my cashbox of sunlight my volcanic fruit
my laugh of a secluded lake where absent-minded prophets
    always remember to come and drown
my high tide of black-currant my mushroom butterfly
my waterfall as blue as the ground-swell that begins the spring
my coral revolver whose mouth attracts me like the eye of a
    glistening wet well
as glazed over as the mirror in which you contemplate the flight
    of the hummingbirds of your own eyes
lost in a display case for white linen whose frame is made entirely out
    of mummies
I love you

Benjamin Péret
Translated by Michael Benedikt

"Hello" is an example of how surrealistic images force a reader to interpret them as metaphor. Péret states no tenor, and his poem seems at first reading to be absolute nonsense. But the last line, "I love you," allows the reader to guess a tenor. Each of the first eighteen lines presents an apparently unrelated absurdity, some kind of explosion or horror or delight, as if the poet is saying, "Loving you makes me tremble all over." Is the possible tenor, "To love is to feel idiotically happy"? I say *possible tenor* because the poet has deliberately refused to tie the meaning into a hard knot at the end. If he means that love is an explosion, he wants to make it explode in his reader. And explosions don't explain.

EXERCISES

1. Find the tenors and vehicles in the following poems:

THE BULL MOSES

A hoist up and I could lean over
The upper edge of the high half-door,
My left foot ledged on the hinge, and look in at the byre's
Blaze of darkness: a sudden shut-eyed look
Backward into the head.
                    Blackness is depth
Beyond star. But the warm weight of his breathing,
The ammoniac reek of his litter, the hotly-tongued
Mash of his cud, steamed against me.
Then, slowly, as onto the mind's eye —
The brow like masonry, the deep-keeled neck:
Something come up there onto the brink of the gulf,
Hadn't heard of the world, too deep in itself to be called to,
Stood in sleep. He would swing his muzzle at a fly
But the square of sky where I hung, shouting, waving,
Was nothing to him; nothing of our light
Found any reflection in him.
                    Each dusk the farmer led him
Down to the pond to drink and smell the air,
And he took no pace but the farmer
Led him to take it, as if he knew nothing
Of the ages and continents of his fathers,
Shut, while he wombed, to a dark shed
And steps between his door and the duckpond;
The weight of the sun and the moon and the world hammered
To a ring of brass through his nostrils.
                    He would raise
His streaming muzzle and look out over the meadows,
But the grasses whispered nothing awake, the fetch
Of the distance drew nothing to momentum
In the locked black of his powers. He came strolling gently back,
Paused neither toward the pigpens on his right,

Nor toward the cow-byres on his left: something
Deliberate in his leisure, some beheld future
Founding in his quiet.
                                        I kept the door wide,
Closed it after him and pushed the bolt.

TED HUGHES

THE YAWN OF YAWNS

Once upon a time there was a yawn
Neither under the palate nor under the hat
Neither in the mouth nor in anything else

It was bigger than all
Bigger than its own bigness

From time to time
Its dense night its hopeless night
Would glitter hopelessly here and there
You'd think there were stars

Once upon a time there was a yawn
Boring as any yawn
And it still seems to go on and on

VASKO POPA
Translated by Charles Simic

DIVING INTO THE WRECK

First having read the book of myths,
and loaded the camera,
and checked the edge of the knife-blade,
I put on
the body-armor of black rubber
the absurd flippers
the grave and awkward mask.
I am having to do this
not like Cousteau with his
assiduous team
aboard the sun-flooded schooner
but here alone.

Metaphor

There is a ladder.
The ladder is always there
hanging innocently
close to the side of the schooner.
We know what it is for,
we who have used it.
Otherwise
it's a piece of maritime floss
some sundry equipment.

I go down.
Rung after rung and still
the oxygen immerses me
the blue light
the clear atoms
of our upper air.
I go down.
My flippers cripple me,
I crawl like an insect down the ladder
and there is no-one
to tell me when the ocean
will begin.

First the air is blue and then
it is bluer and then green and then
black I am blacking out and yet
my mask is powerful
it pumps my blood with power.
The sea is another story
the sea is not a question of power
I have to learn alone
to turn my body without force
in the deep element.

And now: it is easy to forget
what I came for
among so many who have always
lived here
swaying their crenellated fans
between the reefs
and besides
you breathe differently down here.

I came to explore the wreck.
The words are purposes.
The words are maps.
I came to see the damage that was done
and the treasures that prevail.
I stroke the beam of my lamp
slowly along the flank
of something more permanent
than fish or weed

the thing I came for:
the wreck and not the story of the wreck
the thing itself and not the myth
the drowned face always staring
towards the sun
the evidence of damage
worn by salt and sway into this threadbare beauty
the ribs of the disaster curving their assertion
among the tentative haunters.

This is the place.
And I am here, the mermaid whose dark hair
streams black, the merman in his armored body.
We circle silently
about the wreck
we dive into the hold.
I am she: I am he

whose drowned face sleeps with open eyes
as figurehead
whose breasts still bear the stress
whose silver, copper, golden cargo lies
obscurely inside barrels
half-wedged and left to rot
we are the half-destroyed instruments
that once held to a course
the water-eaten log
the fouled compass

We are, I am, you are
by cowardice or courage
the one who find our way
back to this scene
carrying a knife, a camera,
a book of myths
in which
our names do not appear.

ADRIENNE RICH

2. Free associate two pages of impossible animals. Have no other guide than to make them as absurd as you can. Let cool. Come back later and see if you can detect any resemblance among them. Select and sequence to emphasize the resemblance. Ask the class if your surrealistic sequence, your vehicle, suggests a possible tenor.
3. Answer the following questions by free associating a page or two of answers to each:
   a. What happens when you squeeze a ring?
   b. Can you fold a cloud?
   c. What are buckeyes (or smooth stones or feathers or scissors) for?

   Select and sequence one of these into a poem. Have *ring, cloud,* or *buckeyes* (etc.) become the vehicles for possible tenors in your poem?
4. Complete one of the following statements with a page or two of free association:
   a. I crawled down a long, dark, curving pipe. Suddenly, a bright, round opening. I saw —
   b. I reached my arm down into the hole, down, down, as far as my elbow, as far as my shoulder, and I felt —

   Select and sequence one of these free associations into a poem. In your final sequence do any of the literal details, such as *crawl, dark, pipe* or *reach, hole, down* suggest other than literal meanings?

part three

poets on their own

Now that you have learned how poems can be invited and how to select and sequence the resulting raw material by the principles of *concreteness, structure, rhythm, sound, multiple meaning*, and *metaphor*, you have all the material and tools that any poet has ever had. The rest is practice, and it will take the rest of your life. You will develop your own preferred time, place, and triggering devices for inviting the poem; your own favorite subjects and attitudes; your own preferred sounds, rhythms, and shapes; your own fondness for much multiplicity or little, for understated, barely perceptible metaphors or wildly surrealistic ones — in other words, your own poetic voice, which may be soft or loud, dogmatic or tentative, relaxed or tense, like your speaking voice. You will undoubtedly change, as gradually and imperceptibly as your appearance changes, but noticeably when you compare your earlier poems with your more recent ones. The power and distinction of your poetry will grow as your perception grows.

But to ensure this growth you will need to practice the poetic voice as steadily as you would the singing voice. The best tools for strengthening that voice are the *journal*, the *library*, and the *workshop*.

THE JOURNAL

The poet's journal is not a neat diary that can be kept in a bound notebook, with a dated and gold-edged page for each day. It is not a record of your engagements and expenses or a group of careful sentences and paragraphs interpreting events. It is more like a middle drawer, into which you put miscellaneous things that might come in handy some day — stray screws, bits of string, rubber bands, programs from plays or concerts you enjoyed, letters from people you like and intend to answer some day, half a pair of gloves you're still hoping to find the mate for, half a stick of chewing gum — that sort of thing: tangible, incomplete, suggestive.

The journal is a middle drawer of words — words read and overheard, words you would have said to someone if you'd thought of them in time, words you've invited by free association, beginnings of poems that didn't make it or haven't yet made it, drafts after drafts in all their messiness of poems that finally did make it, exercises, word pictures, brief, neat quotations — all fragmentary stuff — your private middle drawer with no one looking over your shoulder. The most useful journal will have collected something nearly every day. If you wait for the urge to write something down, you may wait weeks or months. But if you sit down every day at six A.M. or right after lunch or just before bed or while riding the bus, and start putting down *anything* that pops into your mind or that you overhear or see passing, your thoughts and sensations will soon form the habit of drifting onto the page. You don't need to read them over or evaluate them more than once a week. If they stand for concrete bits of experience, they'll recall the surroundings and feelings of the rest of the experience whenever you read them again.

For keeping the journal I'd recommend a looseleaf notebook, standard size, with pages and looseleaf pockets. A smaller notebook or pad can be carried in your pocket or purse for those moments in the elevator or waiting at the stoplight when a phrase or a glimpse needs to be put down before it's lost. These can be torn out or off and inserted in the journal's pockets later. When the journal gets too heavy, the earlier pages and pockets can be removed and stored. Never throw them out. Even if you gradually stop looking for usable scraps in the older parts, you, or perhaps your biographer, may someday want to see where you came from. Or some scrap you'd long forgotten might strike you freshly.

A large proportion of professional poets keep some equivalent of a journal, though the fragments may be in shoeboxes or under rubber bands as often as in notebooks. Louis Simpson's poem "The Hour of Feeling,"[1] for example, came partly from such notebook entries.

THE HOUR OF FEELING

Love, now a universal birth,
From heart to heart is stealing,
From earth to man, from man to earth:
— It is the hour of feeling.
Wordsworth, "To My Sister"

A woman speaks:
"I hear you were in San Francisco.
What did they tell you about me?"

She begins to tremble. I can hear the sound
her elbow made, rapping on wood.
It was something to see and to hear —
not like the words that pass for life,
things you read about in the papers.

[1] The information about Simpson's, Wilbur's, Bell's, and Klappert's journals and their worksheets is from *50 Contemporary Poets*, ed. A. Turner (New York: Longman, 1977).

People who read a deeper significance
into everything, every whisper...
who believe that a knife crossed with a fork
are a signal... by the sheer intensity
of their feeling leave an impression.

And with her, tangled in her hair,
came the atmosphere, four walls,
the avenues of the city
at twilight, the lights going on.

When I left I started to walk.
Once I stopped to look at a window
displaying ice skates and skis.
At another with Florsheim shoes...

Thanks to the emotion with which she spoke
I can see half of Manhattan,
the canyons and the avenues.

There are signs high in the air
above Times Square and the vicinity:
a sign for Schenley's Whiskey,
for Admiral Television,
and a sign saying Millitag, whatever that means.

I can see over to Brooklyn and Jersey,
and beyond there are meadows,
and mountains and plains.

LOUIS SIMPSON

The poem began with an experience: living in New York and working as an editor in a publishing house. One day a woman came in to pick up a manuscript that had been rejected. It was a peculiar piece of writing. She had invented a machine for choosing a mate. It looked like the electric chair. You put your prospective partner in it and the pointer swung to a number. Then you made some calculations. After that you were supposed to consult astrological charts. Finally you would consider whether you were compatible. The whole thing was ridiculous. The woman, however, did not look like the kind of eccentric you might have expected. She was about thirty, red-haired, slender — in fact, quite attractive.

I explained to her why we couldn't publish the manuscript. Then she started to tremble — her elbow rapped on the desk as it does in the poem. I saw that the situation was getting out of hand and tried to calm her down. Then she said, "I hear you were in San Francisco. What did they tell you about me?" I had just come back from a short vacation in San Francisco; she had been told I was there when she called to find out the fate of the manuscript. I saw that I had to deal with a person who was not sane. I wasn't the only one to see it. There was a woman sharing my office; she saw what was up and stayed at her desk during our interview, so as to be a witness if one were needed. At the end the woman with the mating machine took her manuscript and left. I was glad to see her go.

As I say in the poem, such people "by the sheer intensity of their feeling leave an impression." The impression was indelibly etched on my consciousness. A few years ago I began trying to write poetry about this period of my life. In these poems I set out to record images of Manhattan and the atmosphere of the city. I tried to work in this episode in my descriptions. The trouble was, I couldn't see what made this episode and one or two others hang together. It isn't enough to describe, you have to know why. Finally I saw what linked this character and the others: it was a feeling in myself, a sympathy I had for them. The insane view held by this woman was, in its way, an act of poetic imagination. She wished to make events in the real world conform to her vision of things. The doctors' name for her condition was paranoia.

The actual writing of the poem, as with most of my poems, took years. I had no idea how it would work out; I had some images and clusters of lines that I would push around. Sometimes I would think I had a poem in view, then it would disintegrate. I would be ashamed to have people see just how hard it is for me to finish what I consider a real poem. Some of my contemporaries don't have this problem: they write down whatever they feel like writing, hardly revise, if indeed they revise at all, and publish it right away. Some of them are able to publish a book every year or two. It takes me five or six years to finish a book of poems.

I saw the woman in the poem in the early 1950s. The images of New York were accumulated over a span of years. Here is a page from a notebook I kept. You will see the bearing this has on material in the poem.

13 Nov. 1962. Monday

B'way & 42nd St. looking North (at my back, Crossroads Cafe).
Distance: Canadian Club
Admiral Television Appliances

N. E. corner: Florsheim (on corner)
Books/Souvenirs
Trans Continental Airlines Agency
Globe: Exclusive New York Showing: *No Morals/*

Midnight Frolics — strictly adults only
— above, Times Square Bowling Lanes

To West (7th Ave)
Rialto: First New York showing: *West End Jungle, the film that London banned — adults only — with Naked Terror*

Cameras Kodak Films
Records Columbia Records

These notes were a source not only of *The Hour of Feeling* but of two other poems as well, *The Rejected* and *The Springs at Gadara* It sometimes happens that many things are conceived at once.

Here is another entry from the notebook, two pages further on. Again, you will see the connection with *The Hour of Feeling*.

42nd bet B'way & Ave. of the Americas

Sweetville candy U. S. A. nuts
Ice skates golf hunting ski equipment
American Irving Savings Time
time temperature
12 27 46
flashes off flashes on

These notes proved useful — notes aren't always useful, they can be a waste of time. But what was much more important in writing about New York was to relive the period imaginatively. This required "immersion." I would imagine myself there, immerse myself in the atmosphere of the time and place, try to see what was significant, concentrate on certain images and eliminate others, and arrive finally at my true feeling about the experience. This is the way I write poetry.

Richard Wilbur traces the growth of his poem "The Eye" to scraps of paper on which he had jotted, as much as four years before writing the poem, prose statements such as this:

One is consciousness, and others are body; one sees them with creased necks in the next row in the theatre, one sees them convulse as they belch, one sees them sleeping with their mouths open in public conveyances.... Even in "love" this can be, that one is the ringmaster and someone else the beast...."

Another scrap contains the first three words of a poem that "got no farther." "The Eye" came only after the experience of looking through binoculars at people in a Carribean resort:

> Evidently I had not wanted to write a poem . . . by 'deciding on a theme and seeking to embody it,' and therefore the essayistic jottings I had earlier made did not conduce to a poem. Approaching the theme through a single situation rich in physical details, and full of reactions and self-judgments, was apparently more appealing, since a poem came of it.

It was another year and a half before he actually began to write the poem.

THE EYE

". . . all this beastly seeing." — D.H. Lawrence

I

One morning in St. Thomas, when I tried
Our host's binoculars, what was magnified?
In the green slopes about us, only green,
Brisked into fronds and paddles, could be seen,
Till by a lunging focus I was shown
Some portion of a terrace like our own.
Someone with ankles crossed, in tennis shoes,
Was turning sun-blank pages of the news,
To whom in time came espadrilles of pink
Bearing a tall and fruit-crowned tropic drink.
How long I witnessed, missing not a sip! —
Then, scanning down through photons to a ship
In the blue bay, spelt out along the bow
The queenly legend of her name; and now
Followed her shuttling lighter as it bore
Her jounced, gay charges landward to explore
Charlotte Amalie, with its duty-free
Leicas, binoculars, and jewelry.
What kept me goggling all that hour? The nice
Discernment of a lime or lemon slice?
A hope of lewd espials? An astounded
Sense of the import of a thing surrounded —
Of what a Z or almond-leaf became
Within the sudden premise of a frame?
All these, and that my eye should flutter there,

By shrewd promotion, in the outstretched air,
An unseen genius of the middle distance,
Giddy with godhead or with nonexistence.

II

Preserve us, Lucy,
From the eye's nonsense, you by whom
Benighted Dante was beheld,
To whom he was beholden.

If the salesman's head
Rolls on the seat-back of the bus
In ugly sleep, his open mouth
Banjo-strung with spittle,

Forbid my vision
To take itself for a curious angel.
Remind me that I am here in body,
A passenger, and rumpled.

Charge me to see
In all bodies the beat of spirit,
Not merely in the *tout en l'air*
Or double pike with layout

But in the strong,
Shouldering gait of the legless man,
The calm walk of the blind young woman
Whose cane touches the curbstone.

Correct my view
That the far mountain is much diminished,
That the fovea is prime composer,
That the lid's closure frees me.

Let me be touched
By the alien hands of love forever,
That this eye not be folly's loophole
But giver of due regard.

RICHARD WILBUR

John Woods' poem "The Five Dreams" was generated by a passage from Camus' *The Guest*. He says, "I wrote the Camus passage in a journal several years ago, feeling that there was something about its gravity that would be a source." John Haines speaks of finding a single grave beside an Alaskan highway:

> I think I may have written something in one of the notebooks I habitually have around, either then or later on that evening when we camped. The earliest things I have are some scribbles on a sheet of looseleaf paper, noting details of the place and the dates. Much of the fifth stanza and the last half-dozen lines of the poem are already there.

Peter Klappert keeps a commonplace book, "a huge collection of quotations and snippets from things I read, anything from single words to long philosophical and descriptive passages."

These professionals invite poems by noticing, recording, saving, and rereading bits of observation in hopes that some felt idea will occur to them. To read a journal full of concreteness is a way of free associating. The poets' deepest present concerns at any moment dictate what they notice.

EXERCISES

1. Read the following sample page from a poet's journal *fast*, underlining the six to a dozen items that intrigue you most. Sequence these (and additional ones that may occur to you as you go along) into a tentative first draft of a felt idea. Revise into a poem. Put aside for a week. Revise again.

IMPOSSIBLE FACES

Glue, a big pool of it — raisins that move
pointy horns, a pig's snout, no chin — Is that God?
a black hole fallen in
the swing — legs running under it
the Cheshire Cat gone out — or flickering
pumpkins, with tall candle eyes
long, long strings of islets, laceless
a crocheted rose, needles for lips
Bring a rope, let me braid it

any thing empty, anything round
anything — I'll put in the nose and eyes — a vacuum mouth
foot soles — blind
a hat — any hat, cap, brim
lock, clamp four seasons in it — omit the ears
black face, running at the edges
any open mouth — teeth for eyes, teeth for chin
saucers of cream, oystershells, rocks with drill holes
banks under holes
in one eye a chipmunk, in one a weasel
the sand is a lip — some beast coming out
Now listen, every head's a mouth — all praying for me? For me?
piano keys lisp, spit under my thumb
hankies for organ mouths — I must embroider some
a pot of stew — onions for eyes, carrots for ears, a turnip with gravy
    running off it.
Cut the leaves around the carrot. Feather-cut will do
Samson — cut the rutabaga's hair for Samson.
The stick has a fork, legs, but the face is leaves — no nose — no eyes
Blanket over, beads below; who knows what that is?
I'd guess a canon ball, a roc's egg, a wooden nose, Pinocchio.

2. Select a time and place where you can be alone for at least a half hour every day. Free associate there, without any purpose in mind. Just talk to yourself and record every pointless, throwaway word that comes into your mind. Don't reread until you have been doing it for a week. Then read all the week's jottings together and see if anything interests or surprises you. Do any of the items recur? Do they form the pattern of a felt idea? If so, edit them into a poem. If not, try another week. This time invite bits of concrete experience by starting off with a concrete word: the name of something you see in your lap, in your room, out the window. Or take the first concrete word you put your finger on when you shut your eyes and open a dictionary — anything to start you talking to yourself.

THE LIBRARY

No poet can be the first or only one. Your original idea of what a poet does came from a book or a performance — your *Mother Goose*, your nursery rhyme records, the songs your mother or sitter sang to you, songs you heard on radio or TV. You soon formed the idea that a poem is a word thing in rhythm and rhyme that can be said or sung, usually to music. You wanted to make one of those. Your first poems were probably made-up, imitative new stanzas to songs you already knew.

Your concept of what poetry is can grow only as you read more poetry, imitate what appeals to you in it, and gradually exceed and modify it according to your needs. The same process takes place in learning other skills. The first time a woman makes a pie crust she does exactly what the directions or her sister or mother tells her to do; by the time she has baked twenty pies, she takes a short cut or two, introduces a little more or a little less flour, and rolls it with her own peculiar turn of wrist. After several years of this, no one would mistake her pie for anyone else's.

In poetry the process is slower. There are more varieties of poems than pie crusts, centuries of recipes, and all the best examples are still around to be tasted. Also, the maturing poet's taste buds keep changing. The library and the bookstore will be your tasting places. You need to look in both books and magazines for single poems that attract your attention, in any way whatever. If you notice one, if you want to read it again, you need to note the author's name and look up other poems by the same person. If you find that as much as one-fourth of those also catch and hold your attention, you need to ask yourself what combination of subject, felt idea, and technique makes that strong initial attraction (or repulsion). Is it something you yourself have been trying to do in your own poems? What would happen if you tried it? If it doesn't suit your voice, and it may not, you will be able to recognize the fact in direct proportion to how deeply you have analyzed the author's work; if it does suit, your next step is to introduce it gradually into your poems.

Young poets are sometimes afraid of imitation. They fear they will become clones or weak facsimiles of someone else, but they needn't worry. They will probably not be able to imitate the complex of felt idea and voice that identifies any of the master poets at once. At most they can try on a form or a way of looking at a particular subject or a kind of metaphor or a turn of phrase. If it fits, they should probably adopt it. If it doesn't, they'll discard it as soon as they try another. A poet probably *can't* jell in another's mold. Meanwhile, to try on any aspect of another's language is to gain more understanding of what language can do and more control of one's own.

EXERCISES

Write one or more suitable stanzas for the following poems, then ask yourself what in the first stanzas determined your choices of themes, tones, and forms for your additions.

THE DYING COWBOY

As I rode out by Tom Sherman's bar-room,
As I rode out so early one day,
'Twas there I espied a handsome young cowboy,
All dressed in white linen, all clothed for the grave.

"I see by your outfit that you are a cowboy,"
These words he did say as I boldly stepped by.
"Come sit down beside me and hear my sad story,
For I'm shot in the breast and I know I must die.

EIGHT

On the first branch a ball,
a greasy black tennis ball —
soft, with a sort of hair growing off it.

On the next branch a leg
wedged into the crotch,
a gray leg;
I climb around it.

OCCUPATIONAL HAZARDS

Butcher

If I want to go to pieces
I can do that. When I try
to pull myself together
I get sausage.

Bakers

Can't be choosers. Rising
from a white bed, from dreams
of kings, bright cities, buttocks,
to see the moon by daylight.

Tailor

It's not the way the needle
drags the poor thread around.
It's sewing the monster together,
my misshapen son.

The process of finding your own poetic voice will be helped by some critical training, such as courses in individual poets or the poetry of a historical period. The relevance of such courses is shown by the recurrence of the same themes, characters, stories, and techniques in fresh contexts and with equal or greater power in any anthology of English poetry, up to and including the present. Consider, for example (in Poems for Further Discussion), the ways in which Marlowe (1600), Ralegh (1600), Donne (1612), C. Day Lewis (1935), and Louis Simpson (1959) have said quite different things in their poems on the theme of "Come live with me and be my love"; or with what variety of theme and tone Empson's "Missing Dates," Dylan Thomas's "Do Not Go Gentle into That Good Night," and Roethke's "The Waking" have used the fixed French form of the villanelle[2]; or how Wilbur's "Love Calls Us to the Things of This World," Shakespeare's "My Mistress' Eyes Are Nothing Like the Sun," Jonson's "Still to Be Neat," Herrick's "Delight in Disorder," and Hopkins' "Pied Beauty" have variously celebrated the beauty of imperfection; or how Marlowe's "Was This the Face That Launched a Thousand Ships?," Landor's "Past Ruined Ilion Helen Lives," Poe's "To Helen," H. D's "Helen," and Yeats' "When Helen Lived" have depended on the legend of Helen of Troy.

A poet who is serious about becoming one must know the competition. English poetry has sources in Hebrew psalms, African chants, Norse sagas, Oriental court poetry, American Indian religious rituals, to name

[2] *Villanelle*: poem of five three-line stanzas, in which the first and third lines of the first stanza are repeated alternately as the last line of each stanza; and one four-line stanza, which repeats both. Rhyme pattern: aba (5), abaa.

only some. A lifetime of reading is not long enough to take full advantage of poetry's history. A poet who writes every day should read every day.

EXERCISES

1. Make one of the comparisons mentioned two paragraphs above to test your ability to detect similarity and difference in the ways that different personalities and historical periods use the same theme, character, situation, or verse form.
2. Choose one of the following poems and write a poem of your own that imitates its theme, tone, or form on a similar, but not identical, subject: imitate Milton's "On the Late Massacre in Piedmont" on a contemporary outrage against human rights; or write your own sequel to the line "Come live with me and be my love"; or write your own idea of the Second Coming in imitation of Yeats' "The Second Coming" (p. 194); or make a ballad from a current newsworthy murder, in the same verse form as "Frankie and Johnny" (p. 139).

THE WORKSHOP

Poets often tell you that they are writing only for themselves. They love the triumph of making words "come right," of being able to read the finished poem over and surprise and please themselves again and again. If they admit to wanting an audience, they usually see an idealized self as their reader or listener. But they are fooling themselves if they say they are speaking to just one of those ideal selves. They hope and suspect that this self occurs in other people. Indeed they know that some part of that self occurs in everyone, and are tempted to attract and surprise as many of those as possible.

Eventually, of course, they hope their audience will be the market. But how do they get into the market? That is a Catch-22 question. Poems are not ready for the market until at least some readers have agreed that they are ripe enough, firm enough, shapely enough, and fresh enough to compete with other poems already in the market stalls. If poems were fruit, poets would not only taste them and cultivate them themselves, but ask the opinions of family, friends, and passers-by at different stages of their growth. Beginning poets are wise to try their poems in a workshop.

A workshop is a group of poets who gather at regular intervals to help edit one another's poems. It may be held as a class, with a teacher and credits and textbook, or it may be an irregular gathering of friends in someone's living room. Depending on the poetic and critical skills of the poets and on their personal respect for each other, the workshop may be a grubby fight, a dull waste of time, or a valuable tool for teaching poets their trade.

Ideally, one or more of the members should be skilled and published poets and critics already. I say poets *and* critics; skilled poets are nearly always skilled critics too. If they have become skilled poets without extensive analysis (criticism) of their own poems and those of others, they will be of little use in a workshop. They will be able to recognise *that* a poem doesn't work but will have no idea *why*, or will have a vague idea why but no critical vocabulary or analytical habits to help them explain why. On the other hand, critics may have complete academic knowledge of what makes poems work but lack the awareness of ear and eye and the ability to make imaginative leaps that will put them inside a beginner's poem and show its possibilities. Those workshop members who combine critical skill with imagination should also be secure enough to be generous. Although uncritical praise from family or friends can be stifling, some specific discriminating praise can help a poet as much as corrections can. Criticism should encourage, not intimidate. A cutting remark from an expert can make a beginning poet stop writing for good.

A workshop serves best when it contains a core of six to a dozen poets who come regularly. The poems should be neither in first draft nor finished form. They should be duplicated and distributed to the members several days in advance, so that they can be read several times by each poet critic and some of the most essential comments planned in advance. First reactions off the top of the head seldom get to the root of a poem's problems. If you put a key question or two on the worksheet, you will prevent the helpless O-Lord-what-can-I-say-about-this-one reaction.

Criticism should start with the question, "What is the felt idea (point, theme, thrust)? What is the poem trying to do or be?" If the group answers "I don't know," that is the central problem. No other criticism will be relevant if it doesn't help the poem get where it's going. Often as not, authors will admit that they don't know where a poem is going either. If so, the rest of that poem's workshop time (twenty minutes is enough for one poem at one session) should be spent in suggesting and testing possible threads of meaning.

If the felt idea is identified early, the poem's structure, rhythm, and sound should next be examined to see if they give fullest support to the felt idea. Has the poet used enough concreteness or risked abstraction successfully? Has he used enough syntactical glue? Is she in control of her multiple meanings? Are the metaphors alive? Not all of these will need equal attention. Concentrate on the fundamentals. If a line is a cliché, it doesn't matter whether its rhythm and sound are perfect; it must be rephrased freshly. If a multiple meaning or a metaphor contradicts what the poet is trying to do, it doesn't matter that it is brilliantly original; it must come out.

Every member of a workshop is a teacher and a student of every other member. Each soon learns that X's praise means that the poem is too obvious, that Y will always put a finger on weak metaphors, that Z has a nose for clichés, or that R finds implications of idea that the author didn't intend and doesn't want. The poets' ability to profit from a workshop will grow as their skill grows.

One workshop may not be enough for you. Some poets belong to two at once; some move from one university writing program to another to work with different professional poets. Poets outgrow workshops; their membership changes and with it their chemistry. One year a certain workshop may help and challenge you; another year it may stifle you. You may want to return to the same one after several years' absence or check in only once in four or five meetings. Use them only as long as the poet critics see something more or less or different in your poems from what you see. Use them only to extend your ability to alert a reader.

EXERCISES

1. The following poems comprise the worksheet of a public, free monthly workshop composed of college students, teachers, homemakers, senior citizens, and business executives — some of them beginners, some hobbyists, some published poets. Prepare to join a twenty-minute discussion of each poem by first identifying the felt idea, then writing down two or three of the fundamental criticisms that would be of most use to each poet in revising his or her poem:

APPLES NAMED PAULA

june july green
nubs among leaves
bitter to bite

tossed by wind
they hold on
rain and sun

till they show
their bright ready
plump for hands

and fill rooms
with their fall
scent past blossom

incarnate smile
sphere of knowledge
tongue only knows

DOLPHIN ON A TIGHTROPE

Humming a strange tune
in familiar sounds
a dolphin swims toward a
sharp line wedging the
sparkling sun between
sea and sky

swimming too far over the
water into space
the dolphin teeters
the horizon
like a dolphin on a tightrope
a pawn of water and
bright shiny things
just a finslength away

PATRICIA VAIRE

YOU ARE RECORD OF MIND

We hold this key

This key unlocks the book of particles
taken from the shelf of rock
The cover sparkles
when hands rub outer edges
Letters jump from its pages
Its story tells of struggling pigeons
perched on cornices of a holy city
In their rarified air
they strut and they peck
and they proclaim their view
of improved sunsets

This key unlocks the book of stars
fallen from the shelf of wood
The binding collapses
when eyes explode from skulls
Words shine from its pages
Its tale conveys lonely eagles
roosting on branches of a sacred forest
In their lessening air
they fret and they watch
and they see their eggs crushed
at unsuspecting night

This key unlocks the book of flames
oozed from the shelf of bone
The title glistens
when toes move near fire
Sentences burn from its pages
Its lore relates hungry vultures
circling corpses of a blessed realm
In their stinking air
they hover and they descend
and they eat bare ribs
in warm mornings

This key unlocks the book of hearts
stolen from the shelf of blood
The author pulses
when ears end silence
Paragraphs beat from its pages
Its image portrays ghostly thrushes
singing in cages of a heavenly world
In their stifling air
they whistle and they flute
and they drown in red song
until the end of day

This key unlocks the book of You
heaved from the shelf of wind
The reader smiles
when minds touch beyond the church
Poems blow from its pages
Its myth speaks of earthly doves
flying on wings from unknown gods
In their lifting air
they cry and they laugh
and they soar near clouds
until You become them

A (+)

You sting
and I swat
and there is no blood.
You are an asterisk
and a bump that itches.
And I am bloodless,

thickskinned,
an unwilling donor.
What do you want
with such common
stuff anyway? You risk
a Rorschach blot

for the taste of salt,
a warm body, attention.
You cannot think I'm food.

JOHN GABLE

YOU AND I

Inside the basket
we have made
of this house,
you and I.
The delicate coiling
has kept me wound
in you,
the dressing of rooms
has made each corner bare.
The furniture has turned
to glass and now
when you clutch
the arm of the chair
with your hand
like a child's,
the secret held
in the fist,
even your gestures
are transparent.
The image I collect
out of the pieces of you
are gone, like the chair,
shattered.
Now we hold each other.
What our bodies take back
in the aftermath
of the dark
is only their reflection.
So the house
is no longer a basket
and you and I
and the concept
of you and I

have gone into
what seems always
to have been hidden.
You lift your hand
from the chair
and what escapes
is the child
running from the heart.

JILL BIALOSKY

I WRITE BITTER LOVE LYRICS TO A TUNE CALLED "FROSTY MORNING" AND YOU HATE THEM

When you say these lyrics are too chilling,
that no one would choose to be so cold,
I ask if you've ever known a welder
in summer, but I remember all the times
you've told me you've never been in love,
and I wonder if I can ever make you see an abstract.

Look, you wish you lived in the semi-tropics:
you don't even like winter. To you it's a season
to be endured from inside, warm,
looking out through icey ferns.
But can't you imagine it any other way?

I would have you think of the welder
who sweated all summer and loved a woman
who left him in August. Finally it is November.
He can forget all that heat.
At dawn he walks out to embrace the freeze.
He passes your house, and, not seeing you
because the frost blocks the pane,
he begins to sing this song.

ARCH

Rainbow   Fountain
Bear the weight of Caesar and his triumphs
the weight of vision over the depths of error

Eyebrow   seedling   her feet
unmined remainder of a lode
vault

-bishop   -angel   -tempter   -fiend
Arch water without spilling
Arch the infinite over an apple
Span   overreach

2. Divide the class into groups of four or five students. Meet for three or four times as separate workshops outside class and work over poems of yours that you have not already worked over in class. What differences in attitude, severity of criticism, and emphasis on different areas of technique do you notice between your small workshops and the class?
3. Do the above exercise again, dividing into different groups. What differences do you notice in attitude, severity of criticism, and emphasis on different areas of technique between your present small workshops and your former small workshops?

part four

poems for further discussion

FRANKIE AND JOHNNY

Frankie and Johnny were lovers,
    Lordy, how they could love,
Swore to be true to each other,
    True as the starts up above,
        He was her man, but he done her wrong.

Frankie went down to the corner,
    To buy her a bucket of beer,
Frankie says "Mister Bartender,
    Has my lovin' Johnny been here?
        He is my man, but he's doing me wrong."

"I don't want to cause you no trouble
    Don't want to tell you no lie,
I saw your Johnny half-an-hour ago
    Making love to Nelly Bly,
        He is your man, but he's doing you wrong."

Frankie went down to the hotel
    Looked over the transom so high,
There she saw her lovin' Johnny
    Making love to Nelly Bly.
        He was her man; he was doing her wrong.

Frankie threw back her kimono,
    Pulled out her big forty-four;
Rooty-toot-toot: three times she shot
    Right through that hotel door,
        She shot her man, who was doing her wrong.

"Roll me over gently,
    Roll me over slow,
Roll me over on my right side,
    'Cause these bullets hurt me so,
        I was your man, but I done you wrong."

Bring all your rubber-tired hearses
    Bring all your rubber-tired hacks,
They're carrying poor Johnny to the burying ground
    And they ain't gonna bring him back,
        He was her man, but he done her wrong.

Frankie says to the sheriff,
    "What are they going to do?"
The sheriff he said to Frankie,
    "It's the 'lectric chair for you.
        He was your man, and he done you wrong."

"Put me in that dungeon,
    Put me in that cell,
Put me where the northeast wind
    Blows from the southeast corner of hell,
        I shot my man, 'cause he done me wrong."

ANONYMOUS

SANDWICH

Lace and sequins on a muffin
Clouds and violets on salt bread
Thin face between Kielbasi
John and Jane and John again

ANONYMOUS

THE UNKNOWN CITIZEN

(To JS/07/M/378 This Marble Monument Is Erected by the State)

He was found by the Bureau of Statistics to be
One against whom there was no official complaint,
And all the reports on his conduct agree
That, in the modern sense of an old-fashioned word, he was a saint,

For in everything he did he served the Greater Community.
Except for the War till the day he retired
He worked in a factory and never got fired,
But satisfied his employers, Fudge Motors Inc.
Yet he wasn't a scab or odd in his views,
For his Union reports that he paid his dues,
(Our report on his Union shows it was sound)
And our Social Psychology workers found
That he was popular with his mates and liked a drink.
The Press are convinced that he bought a paper every day
And that his reactions to advertisements were normal in every way.
Policies taken out in his name prove that he was fully insured.
And his Health-card shows he was once in hospital but left it cured.
Both Producers Research and High-Grade Living declare
He was fully sensible to the advantages of the Installment Plan
And had everything necessary to the Modern Man,
A phonograph, a radio, a car and a frigidaire.
Our researchers into Public Opinion are content
That he held the proper opinions for the time of year;
When there were peace, he was for peace; when there was war, he went.
He was married and added five children to the population,
Which our Eugenist says was the right number for a parent of his
    generation,
And our teachers report that he never interfered with their education.
Was he free? Was he happy? The question is absurd:
Had anything been wrong, we should certainly have heard.

W. H. AUDEN

EPITAPH ON A TYRANT

Perfection, of a kind, was what he was after,
And the poetry he invented was easy to understand;
He knew human folly like the back of his hand,
And was greatly interested in armies and fleets;
When he laughed, respectable senators burst with laughter,
And when he cried the little children died in the streets.

W. H. AUDEN

THE MORALIST OF BANANAS

A rustle from the vale — the Saint has gone out to the fields again, to the good, clear fields, there to preach a sermon to the bananas about the suggestiveness of their shapes. It's easy to see why he is called the Moralist of Bananas, too. Every few weeks he announces in town that he is going out to have a serious discussion with the bananas, about the bananas, and for the bananas. "Oh, the objectionable banana!" he cries out as he approaches the bunches of bananas, his thin, hairy legs flashing beneath his long white robes, "O bananas, not only are you shaped in a bodily fashion, but you even ripen by turning from an innocent canary yellow, to bright yellow, to orange, and then to bright skin pink! And some of you, losing all control, even turn bright red, with flesh-tones of jet black!" Believe me, when they see the Saint approaching, the field is filled with fleeing figures, and the rustling of the disentangling of the novice lovers who had left the town earlier to test out their loves there beneath the leaves. Oh yes, we country people may appear relatively primitive here beneath our quaint blankets of moss and leaves that excite us so, but at least we can recognize a Saint in a fit when we see one! I myself can even see him from where I'm lying; he is wandering in the wilderness, alone because all the lovers have gone down among the pomegranates, hid among the permissive persimmon groves, or left for the grapes. Yes, yes, I can hear his voice clearly now too, as I lie here in the grass munching on an apple, snugly beside my best beloved. He is miles away from town, in fact miles away from everyone now, preaching with his customary seriousness to the bananas, calling out to the multitude to whom he is angrily referring as his "poor lost brothers."

MICHAEL BENEDIKT

THE TIGER

Tiger, Tiger, burning bright
In the forests of the night,
What immortal hand or eye
Could frame thy fearful symmetry?

In what distant deeps or skies
Burnt the fire of thine eyes?
On what wings dare he aspire?
What the hand dare seize the fire?

And what shoulder and what art,
Could twist the sinews of thy heart?
And when thy heart began to beat,
What dread hand, and what dread feet?

What the hammer? What the chain?
In what furnace was thy brain?
What the anvil? What dread grasp
Dare its deadly terrors clasp?

When the stars threw down their spears
And watered heaven with their tears,
Did he smile his work to see?
Did he who made the Lamb make thee?

Tiger, Tiger, burning bright
In the forests of the night,
What immortal hand or eye
Dare frame thy fearful symmetry?

William Blake

THE CROSSED APPLE

I've come to give you fruit from out my orchard,
Of wide report.
I have trees there that bear me many apples
Of every sort:

Clear, streakéd; red and russet; green and golden;
Sour and sweet.
This apple's from a tree yet unbeholden,
Where two kinds meet, —

So that this side is red without a dapple,
And this side's hue
Is clear and snowy. It's a lovely apple.
It is for you.

Within are five black pips as big as peas,
As you will find,
Potent to breed you five great apple trees
Of varying kind:

To breed you wood for fire, leaves for shade,
Apples for sauce.
Oh, this is a good apple for a maid,
It is a cross,

Fine on the finer, so the flesh is tight,
And grained like silk.
Sweet Burning gave the red side, and the white
Is Meadow Milk.

Eat it; and you will taste more than the fruit:
The blossom, too,
The sun, the air, the darkness at the root,
The rain, the dew,

The earth we came to, and the time we flee,
The fire and the breast.
I claim the white part, maiden, that's for me.
You take the rest.

LOUISE BOGAN

MATTER

No matter what you do
or don't, or imagine,

the tree you live by
is bound to come down.

Maybe not in your lifetime.
Without doubt in its own.

PHILIP BOOTH

THERE IS A GARDEN IN HER FACE

There is a garden in her face,
Where roses and white lilies grow,
A heavenly paradise is that place,
Wherein all pleasant fruits do flow.
There cherries grow, which none may buy
Till "Cherry ripe!" themselves do cry.

Those cherries fairly do enclose
Of orient pearl a double row,
Which when her lovely laughter shows,
They look like rosebuds filled with snow.
Yet them nor peer nor prince can buy,
Till "Cherry ripe!" themselves do cry.

Her eyes like angels watch them still;
Her brows like bended bows do stand,
Threatening with piercing frowns to kill
All that attempt with eye or hand
Those sacred cherries to come nigh,
Till "Cherry ripe!" themselves do cry.

THOMAS CAMPION

"next to of course god america i
love you land of the pilgrims' and so forth oh
say can you see by the dawn's early my
country 'tis of centuries come and go
and are no more what of it we should worry
in every language even deafanddumb
thy sons acclaim your glorious name by gorry
by jingo by gee by gosh by gum
why talk of beauty what could be more beautiful than these heroic happy dead
who rushed like lions to the roaring slaughter
they did not stop to think they died instead
then shall the voice of liberty be mute?"

He spoke. And drank rapidly a glass of water

e. e. cummings

SONGS

I

the
　　sky
　　　　was
can　dy　lu
minous
　　　　edible
spry
　　pinks shy
lemons
greens　coo　l choc
olate
s.

　un der
　a lo
co
mo
　　tive　s pout
　　　　　　　　ing
　　　　　　　　　vi
　　　　　　　　　o
　　　　　　　　　lets

e.e. cummings

if everything happens that can't be done
(and anything's righter
than books
could plan)
the stupidest teacher will almost guess
(with a run
skip
around we go yes)
there's nothing as something as one

one hasn't a why or because or although
(and buds know better
than books
don't grow)
one's anything old being everything new
(with a what
which
around we come who)
one's everyanything so

so world is a leaf so tree is a bough
(and birds sing sweeter
than books
tell how)
so here is away and so your is a my
(with a down
up
around again fly)
forever was never till now

now i love you and you love me
(and books are shuter
than books
can be)
and deep in the high that does nothing but fall
(with a shout
each
around we go all)
there's somebody calling who's we

we're anything brighter than even the sun
(we're everything greater
than books
might mean)
we're everyanything more than believe
(with a spin
leap
alive we're alive)
we're wonderful one times one

e. e. cummings

anyone lived in a pretty how town
(with up so floating many bells down)
spring summer autumn winter
he sang his didn't he danced his did.

Women and men(both little and small)
cared for anyone not at all
they sowed their isn't they reaped their same
sun moon stars rain

children guessed(but only a few
and down they forgot as up they grew
autumn winter spring summer)
that noone loved him more by more

when by now and tree by leaf
she laughed his joy she cried his grief
bird by snow and stir by still
anyone's any was all to her

someones married their everyones
laughed their cryings and did their dance
(sleep wake hope and then)they
said their nevers they slept their dream

stars rain sun moon
(and only the snow can begin to explain
how children are apt to forget to remember
with up so floating many bells down)

one day anyone died i guess
(and noone stooped to kiss his face)
busy folk buried them side by side
little by little and was by was

all by all and deep by deep
and more by more they dream their sleep
noone and anyone earth by april
wish by spirit and if by yes.

Women and men(both dong and ding)
summer autumn winter spring
reaped their sowing and went their came
sun moon stars rain

e. e. cummings

A NARROW FELLOW IN THE GRASS

A narrow Fellow in the Grass
Occasionally rides —
You may have met Him — did you not
His notice sudden is —

The Grass divides as with a Comb —
A spotted shaft is seen —
And then it closes at your feet
And opens further on —

He likes a Boggy Acre
A Floor too cool for Corn —
Yet when a Boy, and Barefoot —
I more than once at Noon

Have passed, I thought, a Whip lash
Unbraiding in the Sun
When stooping to secure it
It wrinkled, and was gone —

Several of Nature's People
I know, and they know me —
I feel for them a transport
Of cordiality —

But never met this Fellow
Attended, or alone
Without a tighter breathing
And Zero at the Bone —

EMILY DICKINSON

THE BAIT

Come live with me, and be my love,
And we will some new pleasures prove,
Of golden sands, and crystal brooks:
With silken lines, and silver hooks.

There will the river whispering run
Warmed by thy eyes, more than the sun.
And there th' enamored fish will stay,
Begging themselves they may betray.

When thou wilt swim in that live bath,
Each fish, which every channel hath,
Will amorously to thee swim,
Gladder to catch thee, than thou him.

If thou to be so seen be'st loath
By sun, or moon, thou dark'nest both,
And if myself have leave to see,
I need not their light, having thee.

Let others freeze with angling reeds,
And cut their legs with shells and weeds,
Or treacherously poor fish beset
With strangling snare, or windowy net.

Let coarse bold hands, from slimy nest
The bedded fish in banks out-wrest;
Or curious traitors, sleave-silk flies,
Bewitch poor fishes' wand'ring eyes.

For thee, thou need'st no such deceit,
For thou thyself art thine own bait;
That fish that is not catched thereby,
Alas, is wiser far than I.

JOHN DONNE

HELEN

All Greece hates
the still eyes in the white face,
the luster as of olives
where she stands,
and the white hands.

All Greece reviles
the wan face when she smiles,
hating it deeper still
when it grows wan and white,
remembering past enchantments
and past ills.

Greece sees unmoved
God's daughter, born of love,
the beauty of cool feet
and slenderest of knees,
could love indeed the maid,
only if she were laid,
white ash amid funereal cypresses.

H. D. (Hilda Doolittle)

SWEENEY AMONG THE NIGHTINGALES

ὤμοι, πέπληγμαι καιρίαν πληγὴν ἔσω.[1]

Apeneck Sweeney spreads his knees
Letting his arms hang down to laugh,
The zebra stripes along his jaw
Swelling to maculate giraffe.

The circles of the stormy moon
Slide westward toward the River Plate,
Death and the Raven[2] drift above
And Sweeney guards the hornéd gate.[3]

[1]King Agamemnon's cry when his adulterous wife, Clytemnestra, stabbed him on his return from the Trojan war: "Alas, I am struck with a mortal blow within."
[2]The constellation Corvus.
[3]The gate through which true dreams come.

Gloomy Orion and the Dog[4]
Are veiled; and hushed the shrunken seas;
The person in the Spanish cape
Tries to sit on Sweeney's knees

Slips and pulls the table cloth
Overturns a coffee-cup,
Reorganized upon the floor
She yawns and draws a stocking up;

The silent man in mocha brown
Sprawls at the window-sill and gapes;
The waiter brings in oranges
Bananas figs and hothouse grapes;

The silent vertebrate in brown
Contracts and concentrates, withdraws;
Rachel *née* Rabinovitch
Tears at the grapes with murderous paws;

She and the lady in the cape
Are suspect, thought to be in league;
Therefore the man with heavy eyes
Declines the gambit, shows fatigue,

Leaves the room and reappears
Outside the window, leaning in,
Branches of wistaria
Circumscribe a golden grin;

The host with someone indistinct
Converses at the door apart,
The nightingales are singing near
The Convent of the Sacred Heart,

And sang within the bloody wood
When Agamemnon cried aloud,
And let their liquid siftings fall
To stain the stiff dishonored shroud.

T. S. Eliot

[4] The constellation Orion and the Dog Star, Sirius.

MISSING DATES

Slowly the poison the whole blood stream fills.
It is not the effort nor the failure tires.
The waste remains, the waste remains and kills.

It is not your system or clear sight that mills
Down small to the consequence a life requires;
Slowly the poison the whole blood stream fills.

They bled an old dog dry yet the exchange rills
Of young dog blood gave but a month's desires
The waste remains, the waste remains and kills.

It is the Chinese tombs and the slag hills
Usurp the soil, and not the soil retires.
Slowly the poison the whole blood stream fills.

Not to have fire is to be a skin that shrills.
The complete fire is death. From partial fires
The waste remains, the waste remains and kills.

It is the poems you have lost, the ills
From missing dates, at which the heart expires.
Slowly the poison the whole blood stream fills.
The waste remains, the waste remains and kills.

William Empson

SILENT POEM

backroad leafmold stonewall chipmunk
underbrush grapevine woodchuck shadblow

woodsmoke cowbarn honeysuckle woodpile
sawhorse bucksaw outhouse wellsweep

backdoor flagstone bulkhead buttermilk
candlestick ragrug firedog brownbread

hilltop outcrop cowbell buttercup
whetstone thunderstorm pitchfork steeplebush

gristmill millstone cornmeal waterwheel
watercress buckwheat firefly jewelweed

gravestone groundpine windbreak bedrock
weathercock snowfall starlight cockcrow

ROBERT FRANCIS

FAMILY IN A YARD

There's not much to go on at first,
a woman sunning, reading a book,
a man in a print shirt staring up
at the weathervane, some drunkenness,
a younger man working on a small boat,
a younger woman wiping a watermelon.

Hands under heads, water creaking.
The first to wake looks up: You
must come to the table at once,
an older woman says, money is lent,
chicken beautifully carved, swallowed.

After the rich cabbage soup, a girl
runs to the back porch to measure
the sofa for a new cushion. How easy
to tell the present from the past.

STUART FRIEBERT

THE STORE

Your father puts his arm around your neck,
then he moves in one giant step to the street,
it's a long street with all kinds of stores,
one of them stands out of the mist, he enters it,
the clip tie is in his pocket, the cream jacket
hangs on a hook, the first thing he does is dust
the perfume counter. Hours later, just before
he casts the red sweeping compound on the floor
and looks for the push broom, your mother comes

in for perfume. She wants nothing else from him
so he makes change and puts the case back in order.

Now comes the sway through the quiet bare store,
the floorboards are sweet and he moves across them,
whispering, shaking. At the display window, his hand
moves out for the switch. Now the lights go out,
now they go on again. They pulse all night long.

Stuart Friebert

RANGE-FINDING

The battle rent a cobweb diamond-strung
And cut a flower beside a groundbird's nest
Before it stained a single human breast.
The stricken flower bent double and so hung.
And still the bird revisited her young.
A butterfly its fall had dispossessed,
A moment sought in air his flower of rest,
Then lightly stooped to it and fluttering clung.
On the bare upland pasture there had spread
O'ernight 'twixt mullein stalks a wheel of thread
And straining cables wet with silver dew.
A sudden passing bullet shook it dry.
The indwelling spider ran to greet the fly,
But finding nothing, sullenly withdrew.

Robert Frost

FULL-CHOKED

Dark faced at the grease rack,
your cousin with a cut hand
and a head cold dug a crowbar
without a chisel point

down through white-centered stonework
and broke an arm,
like a cousin who held bear hounds
in a filling station

when the fins of a turbine
started like shaft-powered shears,
or someone whose full-choke rifle
went off, in mist like your sister

who wore out a grease rack
by giving rides,
with a dark hydraulic lift,
to six people in the front seat,

splashed to the neck with bursts of light.
Someone grinds off the buckshot marks
on the flank of a pickup
and sits down hard,

turning broadside with a rush,
when a cattle truck backfires.
A Confederate monument
frozen foam-white

points out a sister
to the white wings
of cavalry, as they touch
in the Wilderness Campaign

when the sister,
field crow or darter hawk,
freezes like helical gears
in blue light, where your cousin

who splashes a hyacinth
dark piece of studded tin,
a twin-throated carburetor,
with gasoline, lights a match

and freezes like a hawk
or a dog's eyes
when a grandmother
with a sister at a wide ditch

burns a clump of cottonwoods,
as they stood in the Wilderness
Campaign, like the cavalry
whose wings touch across the back

of the white field.
A sister with a deer rifle
points to cottonwoods
foam-studded with the white wings

of forty hens.
Full-choked eyes
in a dog's head
burn like two grandmothers splashed
by detachments of cavalry.

JAN HAAGENSEN

AT SLIM'S RIVER

Past Burwash and the White River delta,
we stopped to read a sign
creaking on its chains in the wind.

I left the car and climbed a grassy bluff,
to a grey cross leaning there
and a name that was peeling away:

"Alexander Clark Fisher.
Born October 1870. Died January 1941."

No weathering sticks from a homestead
remained on that hillside,
no log sill rotting under moss
nor cellarhole filling with rose vines.
Not even the stone ring
of a hunter's fire,

a thin wire flaking in the brush.
Only the red rock piled
to hold the cross, our blue car
standing on the road below,
and a small figure playing there.
The Yukon sunlight warming a land
held long under snow,
and the lake water splashing.

From the narrow bridge in the distance
a windy clatter of iron —
billow of dust on a blind crossing,
but a keen silence behind that wind.

It was June 4, 1973. I was forty-nine.

My ten-year-old daughter
called me from the road:
she had found a rock to keep,

and I went down.

JOHN HAINES

UNDER THE APPLE TREE

I hold an apple, and five worms slip out between my fingers and begin to march toward the ocean.

— Where do you think you're going, worms?
— We are tired of eating apple. We're going fishing!

STRATIS HAVIARAS

STILL LIFE

A smell of leather in the air. When it's hot and humid, old leather softens, revives, gives off a heavy odor, makes me think of cows and horses in the slaughterhouses,

The
war
was
over.

of death by concussion, by hammer and spike behind the ear, by knife where the spine links to the skull, or in the part of the throat where the lump of chewed grass is held for a breath and released.

During the war, the last animals to perish were the horses. As soon as their legs could no longer support them people would kill them, but would find no meat there. Reluctantly, they'd boil the head for some broth, and eat the tongue, the cheeks, parts of the eyes and the brain. There were skulls of horses all over, one in our own yard. Washed from the rain, immaculate skull, teeth resigned, teeth resting on teeth imperceptibly, and in the brain's cave, the grass ascending serenely.

The
fields
were
sown
again
with
grain.
Grand-
mother
placed
that
skull
on
a
post
as
a
scare-
crow.

STRATIS HAVIARAS

DELIGHT IN DISORDER

A sweet disorder in the dress
Kindles in clothes a wantonness.
A lawn about the shoulders thrown
Into a fine distractiön;
An erring lace, which here and there
Enthralls the crimson stomacher,
A cuff neglectful, and thereby
Ribbands to flow confusedly;
A winning wave, deserving note,
In the tempestuous petticoat;
A careless shoestring, in whose tie
I see a wild civility;
Do more bewitch me than when art
Is too precise in every part.

ROBERT HERRICK

PIED BEAUTY

Glory be to God for dappled things —
For skies of couple-color as a brinded cow;
For rose-moles all in stipple upon trout that swim;
Fresh-firecoal chestnut-falls; finches' wings;
Landscape plotted and pieced — fold, fallow, and plow;
And all trades, their gear and tackle and trim.
All things counter, original, spare, strange;
Whatever is fickle, freckled (who knows how?)
With swift, slow; sweet, sour; adazzle, dim;
He fathers-forth whose beauty is past change:
Praise him.

GERARD MANLEY HOPKINS

WOOD

Reliquaries the size of samovars holding bits of the true cross, so crusted over with gold and jewels you'd never notice the toothpick of holy wood if it weren't smack in the center, takes you back to faith in miracles, times they'd pray to that fragment of Calvary, how he got there, from planing wood in the shop, pushing off the long fragrant curls, the shavings, the sawdust that got in your hair and stung your nose, the fresh droplets of sap on the cut tree, sticky as honey and bright as amber, that's memory, a fly trapped forever like a star in a sapphire, night sky over the olive grove at Gethsemane, he put his hand on the trunk, called for his father, I called, stacking wood until my arms were frozen, loading it in the old horse trailer, my father swinging the angry buzz saw, I got a sliver in my palm, cried, we went home with wood, burned it all winter, the glowing logs eaten away by flame, an incandescent heart that looked like miniature cities sacked and smoldering, that's memory, wood, the stick in your hand you smack the sheep with and yell at the dogs, we were there, that's memory, the wood that goes into your house, this paper, his cross, the cedar chest of a bride who is buried in a box of pine.

PATRICIA IKEDA

ON MY FIRST DAUGHTER

Here lies, to each her parents' ruth,
Mary, the daughter of their youth;
Yet all heaven's gifts being heaven's due,
It makes the father less to rue.
At six months' end she parted hence
With safety of her innocence;
Whose soul heaven's queen, whose name she bears,
In comfort of her mother's tears,
Hath placed amongst her virgin-train:
Where, while that severed doth remain,
This grave partakes the fleshly birth;
Which cover lightly, gentle earth!

BEN JONSON

STILL TO BE NEAT

Still to be neat, still to be dressed,
As you were going to a feast;
Still to be powdered, still perfumed;
Lady, it is to be presumed,
Though art's hid causes are not found,
All is not sweet, all is not sound.

Give me a look, give me a face
That makes simplicity a grace;
Robes loosely flowing, hair as free;
Such sweet neglect more taketh me
Than all th' adulteries of art.
They strike mine eyes, but not my heart.

BEN JONSON

COUNTING THE MAD

This one was put in a jacket,
This one was sent home,
This one was given bread and meat
But would eat none,
And this one cried No No No No
All day long.

This one looked at the window
As though it were a wall,
This one saw things that were not there,
This one things that were,
And this one cried No No No No
All day long.

This one thought himself a bird,
This one a dog,
And this one thought himself a man,
An ordinary man,
And cried and cried No No No No
All day long.

DONALD JUSTICE

ARS POETICA[5]

The goose that laid the golden egg
Died looking up its crotch
To find out how its sphincter worked.

Would you lay well? Don't watch.

X. J. KENNEDY

[5] "The Art of Poetry," by Horace, Roman poet, 65 B.C. to 8 B.C.

EPITAPH FOR A POSTAL CLERK

Here lies wrapped up tight in sod
Henry Harkins c/o God.
On the day of Resurrection
May be opened for inspection.

X. J. KENNEDY

VARIATIONS ON A THEME BY WILLIAM CARLOS WILLIAMS

1

I chopped down the house that you had been saving to live in next
summer.
I am sorry, but it was morning, and I had nothing to do
and its wooden beams were so inviting.

2

We laughed at the hollyhocks together
and then I sprayed them with lye.
Forgive me. I simply do not know what I am doing.

3

I gave away the money that you had been saving to live on for the next
ten years.
The man who asked for it was shabby
and the firm March wind on the porch was so juicy and cold.

4

Last evening we went dancing and I broke your leg.
Forgive me. I was clumsy, and
I wanted you here in the wards, where I am the doctor!

KENNETH KOCH
(See Williams, p. 192)

SESTINA: AQUA AND AFTER

Over the ancient earth our new babe Aquamarine
walks, afrill in organdy and simple. All
gurgling and alick at the blossomy
bosom. Though not
for long. Nothing is lengthy under the great Bloom except
what comes after

There is the perpetual After,
it will not go away. Baby Aquamarine
don't know that yet. "Great Balls of Bloom,"
says our hero, After. "She's all
right. No iota out of place, not
one." He thinks he'll have this blossom

hot, he is so greedy. And the grass, ablossom,
is his ally, deep. After
the ground gets done, not
one will be left of Aqua
to tell her story. But soft: here she trips, all
right, on hands and knees, the bloom

under her nose. *Smell*, says the worm, *this bloom*!
A rose. And she does, all blossoming
and ready, sniff: not flower, but all
the rank stench of cold below and after
Aqua. "Sweet Jesus!" gulps Aqua
agape. "This is not

for me!" Oh awful, we agree, not
the crawling underbelly of bloom
tamped to a dirge cold packed over Aqua.
Horrible quick her blossom
droops. Dreadful is knowing. Thus After
has her. Though she twists and turns all

ways, there is no getting away from it all.
And there is no not
one bright spot anywhere. After
is everywhere, his cold laughter. "Every bloom
has its worm," he croons. "You will blossom
again, Aquamarine,

though quite differently." Oh she's a sight, Aqua
the blossomy, organdy all raggedy, and not, repeat not
ready to quit this blooming place for lover After.

MARILYN KRYSL

POEM FOR THE LEFT AND RIGHT HANDS

The left hand trails in the water
The right is tying knots

The right stitches a seam
The left sleeps in the silk

The right eats
The left listens under the table

The right swears
The left wears the rings

The right wins, the right loses
The left holds the cards

The left strikes chords while the right
runs, runs   up and down, up and down

and when the right can't sleep and travels around the
    world against the clock
the left is buried

Oh left hand you're so quiet
Do you have children, a dog, mistresses, debts

It's the right that buys the groceries
shifts gears
runs for high office
feeds the baby little silver spoonfuls
It's the right that grabs the knife
to hack off the left hand

The left hand waits
a blind dog

holding in its mouth
the right's glove

The knife falls, clatters
The left hand

is the right's only chance

MARILYN KRYSL

PAST RUINED ILION HELEN LIVES

Past ruined Ilion Helen lives,
   Alcestis rises from the shades;
Verse calls them forth; 'tis verse that gives
   Immortal youth to mortal maids.

Soon shall Oblivion's deepening veil
   Hide all the peopled hills you see,
The gay, the proud, while lovers hail
   In distant ages you and me.

The tear for fading beauty check,
   For passing glory cease to sigh;
One form shall rise above the wreck,
   One name, Ianthe,[6] shall not die.

WALTER SAVAGE LANDOR

[6] Real or imagined friend of Landor.

SONG

Come, live with me and be my love,
And we will all the pleasures prove
Of peace and plenty, bed and board,
That chance employment may afford.

I'll handle dainties on the docks
And thou shalt read of summer frocks:
At evening by the sour canals
We'll hope to hear some madrigals.

Care on thy maiden brow shall put
A wreath of wrinkles, and thy foot
Be shod with pain: not silken dress
But toil shall tire thy loveliness.

Hunger shall make thy modest zone
And cheat fond death of all but bone —
If these delights thy mind may move,
Then live with me and be my love.

C. Day Lewis

WEDDING-RING

My wedding-ring lies in a basket
as if at the bottom of a well.
Nothing will come to fish it back up
and onto my finger again.
                    It lies
among keys to abandoned houses,
nails waiting to be needed and hammered
into some wall,
telephone numbers with no names attached,
idle paperclips.
                    It can't be given away

for fear of bringing ill-luck.
It can't be sold
for the marriage was good in its own
time, though that time is gone.
Could some artificer
beat into it bright stones, transform it
into a dazzling circlet no one could take
for solemn betrothal or to make promises
living will not let them keep? Change it
into a simple gift I could give in friendship?

DENISE LEVERTOV

OPUSCULES

I.

Her fingers are this long: with one hand
she plays the clavichord
and my spine.

II.

Frost-like, dust-like: who
is the inventor of tranquilizers
and will she marry me?

III.

The moths and I, without you,
are hovering around our separate lights.
We are lonely, bloodsore.

IV.

The gullies of your body. Do I think
mnemonically
or are they question marks?

V.

The sole description of my present
state: guarded rapture.

THOMAS LUX

THE PASSIONATE SHEPHERD TO HIS LOVE

Come live with me and be my love,
And we will all the pleasures prove
That valleys, groves, hills, and fields,
Woods, or steepy mountain yields.

And we will sit upon the rocks,
Seeing the shepherds feed their flocks,
By shallow rivers to whose falls
Melodious birds sing madrigals.

And I will make thee beds of roses
And a thousand fragrant posies,
A cap of flowers, and a kirtle
Embroidered all with leaves of myrtle;

A gown made of the finest wool
Which from our pretty lambs we pull;
Fair lined slippers for the cold,
With buckles of the purest gold;

A belt of straw and ivy buds,
With coral clasps and amber studs:
And if these pleasures may thee move,
Come live with me, and be my love.

The shepherd swains shall dance and sing
For thy delight each May morning:
If these delights thy mind may move,
Then live with me and be my love.

CHRISTOPHER MARLOWE

WAS THIS THE FACE THAT LAUNCHED A THOUSAND SHIPS[7]

Was this the face that launched a thousand ships,
And burnt the topless towers of Ilium?

[7] The speaker is Faust, in Marlowe's play *Dr. Faustus.* He has sold his soul to the devil for power and has just conjured up the ghost of Helen of Troy.

Sweet Helen, make me immortal with a kiss!
Her lips suck forth my soul; see where it flies.
Come, Helen, come, give me my soul again.
Here will I dwell, for heaven is in these lips,
And all is dross that is not Helena.
I will be Paris, and for love of thee
Instead of Troy shall Wittenberg be sacked,
And I will combat with weak Menelaus,
And wear thy colors on my pluméd crest.
Yea, I will wound Achilles in the heel,
And then return to Helen for a kiss.
O, thou art fairer than the evening's air,
Clad in the beauty of a thousand stars.
Brighter art thou than flaming Jupiter,
When he appeared to hapless Semele;
More lovely than the monarch of the sky,
In wanton Arethusa's azured arms,
And none but thou shalt be my paramour.

CHRISTOPHER MARLOWE

ON A DROP OF DEW

See how the orient dew,
Shed from the bosom of the morn
  Into the blowing roses,
Yet careless of its mansion new
For the clear region where 'twas born
  Round in itself incloses,
  And in its little globe's extent
Frames as it can its native element;
  How it the purple flow'r does slight,
  Scarce touching where it lies,
But gazing back upon the skies,
  Shines with a mournful light
    Like its own tear,
Because so long divided from the sphere.
  Restless it rolls and unsecure,
    Trembling lest it grow impure,
  Till the warm sun pity its pain,

And to the skies exhale it back again.
    So the soul, that drop, that ray
Of the clear fountain of eternal day,
Could it within the human flower be seen,
    Rememb'ring still its former height,
    Shuns the sweet leaves and blossoms green;
    And, recollecting its own light,
Does, in its pure and circling thoughts, express
The greater Heaven in an Heaven less.
    In how coy a figure wound,
    Every way it turns away;
    So the world excluding round,
    Yet receiving in the day:
    Dark beneath, but bright above,
    Here disdaining, there in love.
  How loose and easy hence to go,
  How girt and ready to ascend;
  Moving but on a point below,
  It all about does upwards bend.
Such did the manna's sacred dew distill,
White and entire, though congealed and chill;
Congealed on earth, but does, dissolving, run
Into the glories of th' almighty sun.

ANDREW MARVELL

THE EGG

Filled with joyful longing I ran across the echoing flagstone terrace and down the broad dressed-stone steps, gradual as a beach, patterned with frost. The sky was an immeasurable shell of shadow. The darkness of the mid-winter season, when the sun never rises but the land never goes out entirely, lay ahead of me, and the empty plains, with thoughts rising out of the sleeping snow, turning to look, reeling, running a few steps, falling again. Far beyond them, the Orphans' Gate. I carried the egg in my left hand, inside the glove, keeping it warm. It meant that I had only one hand to do everything. To hold on. To wave. To fight. To balance. It meant that I would have to let one thing go before I could take up another. I had given up half of myself to hold the egg. And the other half to the journey.

At the foot of the stairs, barely stirring in the twilight, the dog teams were waiting, scores of them, lying in harness, curled on the packed snow. Beside each of them was the driver's round skin tent, and the driver himself, walking up and down to keep warm. Here and there, to what looked like a great distance, fires were fluttering in silence, like votive lights in a cathedral, with dark furred figures huddled near them. As I approached a team its driver would step toward me, grinning fiercely to show what a formidable personage he was, waving his arms to make me realize how he cracked his whip, how he terrified his dogs, how his sled flew on, how the Tooth Spirits, the Eye Spirits, the Hand Spirits, the Bear Evils, the Wolf Evils, the Crow Evils, the Knife-Carrying Ghosts, the Ice-Hollow Ghosts, the Sinew Ghosts, the robbers, and the very stars of wrong courses fled from him. He would open his mouth to show how his voice went out ahead of him to tear into his team like the heat of a building burning behind them. The whips were cracked only in gesture and no voices came from the drivers' mouths, for fear of waking the dogs. I passed driver after driver, each more awesome than the last, each offering me, on his palm, the little bell that was his life — mine for the journey, to return to him only if he brought me safely to the Gate. But I knew not to choose any of these. Ages ago when the first of my kind gave up part of his balance, forever, to pick up a stone, which at once began to be something else, he was rewarded with knowledge. I looked through the crowd until I found, at the edge of the camp, a team of skinny dogs piled in a heap, and a crippled driver limping beside his famished tent.

I stopped there and he hobbled up to me. Nothing about him was ingratiating. Besides being a cripple he had only one eye — his left. And the bell he offered me in his twisted palm was a piece of ice. His sled itself was built with one side different from the other. As I was, now. I nodded my head and he gave a little whistle and the dogs began to stir. And as they did I thought I could feel a stirring in the egg, in my palm — a turning inside it, or even the first faint vibrations of a cry. And once again in my mind I saw — but more clearly than before — the towering columns and the low door of the Orphans' Gate, where no one would know me, but where they would recognize the egg that my mother (who was an orphan) had given to me, and would let me pass through to where it would hatch out and fly before me, pausing, hovering, calling its icy song.

W. S. Merwin

PARADISE LOST (IV, 75–82)

Which way I fly is hell; myself am hell;
And in the lowest deep a lower deep
Still threat'ning to devour me opens wide,
To which the hell I suffer seems a heav'n.
O then at last relent: is there no place
Left for repentance, none for pardon left?
None left but by submission; and that word
Disdain forbids me, and my dread of shame

JOHN MILTON

THE EXTERMINATION OF THE SHY

What of those who freeze at bay,
the white deer?
What will be so remarkable as their stillness?

With what replace
their astonishing swift flight
when they run from us and leap
to the ocean, to the moon?

Or the slowness the shy enjoy when they feel safe
looking up from slow-thinking
gazing, gazing at nothing
releasing their tentative steps,
where will we find such slowness?

VALERY NASH

LUGGAGE

We have no money. We've got lots of luggage. Everything we own we carry along with us in suitcases and laced-up sacks. There are five pieces of luggage.

We arrive in a village. The town hall, the church, an inn with a dining room are all close together.

We ask for work. The inn-keeper says, we have our own unemployed. Men, even.

We spend the night at the inn. The room is cheap. It has a cold tile floor. The tiles are marine-blue and decorated with peat-red. The room has a balcony. The balcony overlooks the marketplace. Down there in the street, continual hawking, haggling, nagging, commending; everything grabbed up and sniffed over. At the fruit-stands red, yellow, and green pyramids tower up. You can smell coffee. The pan of coffee beans at the roasting stand goes around and around. Skinned lambs are carried by on long spits. Gerda and I pack. We carry our luggage down into the courtyard. While I go up to get a heavy suitcase Gerda guards the bags.

I come down with the heavy one. Gerda's gone. I call, Gerda, Gerda. I go upstairs again. I come back down. Two pieces of luggage have disappeared. I call. I look all over the place. I get dragged into the crowd of people in the marketplace. I'm stuck. I scream. I wander around in circles. I go back. Now there are only two pieces of luggage there. I call. I cry. I howl. Gerda comes. She laughs.

I say, Where were you?
She says, in the kitchen, shelling beans.
I say, meanwhile they've stolen our last stitch.
She says, unfortunately not.
I say, the biggest pieces anyway.
She says, we had too much anyhow.
I say, now we have hardly anything.
She says, we've come out ahead all around.
I say, I was counting on that stuff.
She says, either you belong somewhere or why have bags at all.

Gerda and the innkeeper have been married a long time now. They've adopted me. I live in the room with marine-blue and peat-red tiles, and the balcony, over the marketplace.

HELGA M. NOVAK
Translated by Anne Maria Celona

DULCE ET DECORUM EST

Bent double, like old beggars under sacks,
Knock-kneed, coughing like hags, we cursed through sludge,
Till on the haunting flares we turned our backs
And towards our distant rest began to trudge.
Men marched asleep. Many had lost their boots
But limped on, blood-shod. All went lame; all blind;
Drunk with fatigue; deaf even to the hoots
Of disappointed shells that dropped behind.

Gas! Gas! Quick, boys! — An ecstasy of fumbling,
Fitting the clumsy helmets just in time;
But someone still was yelling out and stumbling
And floundering like a man in fire or lime. —
Dim, through the misty panes and thick green light
As under a green sea, I saw him drowning.

In all my dreams, before my helpless sight,
He plunges at me, guttering, choking, drowning.

If in some smothering dreams you too could pace
Behind the wagon that we flung him in,
And watch the white eyes writhing in his face,
His hanging face, like a devil's sick of sin;
If you could hear, at every jolt, the blood
Come gargling from the froth-corrupted lungs,
Obscene as cancer, bitter as the cud
Of vile, incurable sores on innocent tongues, —
My friend, you would not tell with such high zest
To children ardent for some desperate glory,
The old Lie: Dulce et decorum est
Pro patria mori.[8]

WILFRED OWEN

[8] "It is gratifying and fitting to die for one's country." Horace.

NO, THAT CAN'T BE

A big piece has been cut out of the fir hedge now (the garden fence), I wonder who did it and why? Does he know how long hedges take to grow? How often you have to trim them so they grow thick and block things off, cut off the view from here to the road, from the road to the garden and the house?

Now there's nothing more to hide, through the opening in the fence people from far off can see the house and the grounds that were once carefully covered by yellow gravel.

Three people are standing there now, looking at the earth and one of them is drawing something with the tip of his toe; three helpless people watching figures of unspeakable fear drawn in the gravel. For years they've been standing there like that, apparently nothing has changed, except for the piece cut out of the fir hedge, so that you can see them standing there.

ERICA PEDRETTI
Translated by Stuart Friebert

CURB YOUR DOGS AND CHILDREN

Dogs are supposed to be walked on a leash, children by the hand, better yet keep them at home, locked up in the house or the garden in dangerous times. Dogs, roaming around outside without their masters, could find things, drag them back to you, proud to bark, show you what they've got and you'd rather not see it, looking at it turns your stomach and your mind from that moment on.

Children, vagabonding around the place like roaming dogs — and what else do you expect them to do, when else, when else examine this place, the quiet spots in the bushes, the nest of the ring snakes in the watery spots near rivers, the mushroom spots in the woods, children who sneak off from the house and the garden, sauntering along the ditch filled with waste water from the tannery or along the tracks, they could get into something—

it wouldn't be just the trains rumbling by that would throw them down or chase them back screaming to the bloodred trench water and from there over the garden fence down the garden path into the house and up the stairs.

Never again will you have to lock those children in, they'll never willingly leave the house again.

Erica Pedretti
Translated by Stuart Friebert

WHERE ARE YOU

I'd like to speak to you cracked crystal crying like a dog in a
 night of wind-whipped laundry
like a dismasted ship into which the foaming sea-moss is
 beginning to creep
in the very midst of which a cat is mewing because all the rats
 have already left
I'd like to speak to you like a tree uprooted in a windstorm
which has shaken the telegraph wires so much
they look like a scrub-brush for mountains closely resembling the
 lower jaw of a tiger
which is gnashing away at me with the disconcerting sound of a
 bashed-down door
I'd like to speak to you like a subway-train broken down in front
 of the entrance
to a station
into which I stride with a splinter in one toe like a bird in a vine
which is no more capable of yielding the desired wine than a
 closed-off street
where I wander footloose as a wig in a fireplace
which has not warmed anything for so long
it thinks it's a snack-bar counter
on which the rings left by glasses form a long long chain
So I'll simply say to you
that I love you as the kernel of corn loves the sun rising high
 above its blackbird head

Benjamin Péret
Translated by Michael Benedikt

TO HELEN

Helen, thy beauty is to me
 Like those Nicéan barks of yore,
That gently, o'er a perfumed sea,
 The weary, way-worn wanderer bore
 To his own native shore.

On desperate seas long wont to roam,
  Thy hyacinth hair, thy classic face,
Thy Naiad airs have brought me home
  To the glory that was Greece
And the grandeur that was Rome.

Lo! in yon brilliant window-niche
  How statue-like I see thee stand,
  The agate lamp within thy hand!
Ah, Psyche, from the regions which
  Are Holy Land!

EDGAR ALLAN POE

THE WAKING

I wake to sleep, and take my waking slow.
I feel my fate in what I cannot fear.
I learn by going where I have to go.

We think by feeling. What is there to know?
I hear my being dance from ear to ear.
I wake to sleep, and take my waking slow.

Of those so close beside me, which are you?
God bless the Ground! I shall walk softly there,
And learn by going where I have to go.

Light takes the Tree; but who can tell us how?
The lowly worm climbs up a winding stair;
I wake to sleep, and take my waking slow.

Great Nature has another thing to do
To you and me; so take the lively air,
And, lovely, learn by going where to go.

This shaking keeps me steady. I should know.
What falls away is always. And is near.
I wake to sleep, and take my waking slow.
I learn by going where I have to go.

THEODORE ROETHKE

THE NYMPH'S REPLY TO THE SHEPHERD

If all the world and love were young,
And truth in every shepherd's tongue,
These pretty pleasures might me move
To live with thee and be thy love.

Time drives the flocks from field to fold,
When rivers rage, and rocks grow cold,
And Philomel becometh dumb;
The rest complain of cares to come.

The flowers do fade, and wanton fields
To wayward winter reckoning yields:
A honey tongue, a heart of gall,
Is fancy's spring, but sorrow's fall.

Thy gowns, thy shoes, thy beds of roses,
Thy cap, thy kirtle, and thy posies
Soon break, soon wither, soon forgotten;
In folly ripe, in reason rotten.

Thy belt of straw and ivy buds,
Thy coral clasps and amber studs,
All these in me no means can move
To come to thee and be thy love.

But could youth last, and love still breed,
Had joys no date, nor age no need,
Then these delights my mind might move
To live with thee and be thy love.

SIR WALTER RALEGH

BEARS

Wonderful bears that walked my room all night,
Where are you gone, your sleek and fairy fur,
Your eyes' veiled imperious light?

Brown bears as rich as mocha or as musk,
White opalescent bears whose fur stood out
Electric in the deepening dusk,

And great black bears who seemed more blue than black,
More violet than blue against the dark —
Where are you now? upon what track

Mutter your muffled paws, that used to tread
So softly, surely, up the creakless stair
While I lay listening in bed?

When did I lose you? whose have you become?
Why do I wait and wait and never hear
Your thick nocturnal pacing in my room?
My bears, who keeps you now, in pride and fear?

ADRIENNE RICH

HUSH

For My Son

The way a tired Chippewa woman
Who's lost a child gathers up black feathers,
Black quills & leaves
That she wraps & swaddles in a little bale, a shag
Cocoon she carries with her & speaks to always
As if it were the child,
Until she knows the soul has grown fat & clever,
That the child can find its own way at last;
Well, I go everywhere
Picking the dust out of the dust, scraping the breezes
Up off the floor, & gather them into a doll
Of you, to touch at the nape of the neck, to slip
Under my shirt like a rag — the way
Another man's wallet rides above his heart. As you
Cry out, as if calling to a father you conjure
In the paling light, the voice rises, instead, in me.
Nothing stops it, the crying. Not the clove of moon,

Not the woman raking my back with her words. Our letters
Close. Sometimes, you ask
About the world; sometimes, I answer back. Nights
Return you to me for a while, as sleep returns sleep
To a landscape ravaged
& familiar. The dark watermark of your absence, a hush.

DAVID ST. JOHN

MY MISTRESS' EYES ARE NOTHING LIKE THE SUN

My mistress' eyes are nothing like the sun;
Coral is far more red than her lips' red;
If snow be white, why then her breasts are dun;
If hairs be wires, black wires grow on her head.
I have seen roses damasked red and white,
But no such roses see I in her cheeks;
And in some perfumes is there more delight
Than in the breath that from my mistress reeks.
I love to hear her speak, yet well I know
That music hath a far more pleasing sound;
I grant I never saw a goddess go;
My mistress, when she walks, treads on the ground.
And yet, by heaven, I think my love as rare
As any she belied with false compare.

WILLIAM SHAKESPEARE

THE GREEN SHEPHERD

Here sit a shepherd and a shepherdess,
He playing on his melancholy flute;
The sea wind ruffles up her simple dress
And shows the delicacy of her foot.

And there you see Constantinople's wall
With arrows and Greek fire, molten lead;
Down from a turret seven virgins fall,
Hands folded, each one praying on her head.

The shepherd yawns and puts his flute away.
It's time, she murmurs, we were going back.
He offers certain reasons she should stay —
But neither sees the dragon on their track.

A dragon like a car in a garage
Is in the wood, his long tail sticking out.
Here rides St. George swinging his sword and targe,
And sticks the grinning dragon in the snout.

Puffing a smoke ring, like the cigarette
Over Times Square, Sir Dragon snorts his last.
St. George takes off his armor in a sweat.
The Middle Ages have been safely passed.

What is the sail that crosses the still bay,
Unnoticed by the shepherds? It could be
A caravel that's sailing to Cathay,
Westward from Palos on the unknown sea.

But the green shepherd travels in her eye
And whispers nothings in his lady's ear,
And sings a little song, that roses die,
Carpe diem, which she seems pleased to hear.

The vessel they ignored still sails away
So bravely on the water, Westward Ho!
And murdering, in a religious way,
Brings Jesus to the Gulf of Mexico.

Now Portugal is fading, and the state
Of Castile rising purple on Peru;
Now England, now America grows great —
With which these lovers have nothing to do.

What do they care if time, uncompassed, drift
To China, and the crew is a baboon?
But let him whisper always, and her lift
The oceans in her eyelids to the moon.

The dragon rises crackling in the air,
And who is god but Dagon? Wings careen,
Rejoicing, on the Russian hemisphere.
Meanwhile, the shepherd dotes upon her skin.

Old Aristotle, having seen this pass,
From where he studied in the giant's cave,
Went in and shut his book and locked the brass
And lay down with a shudder in his grave.

Louis Simpson

HUNTING, 13

Now I'll also tell what food
we lived on then:

Mescal, yucca fruit, pinyon, acorns,
prickly pear, sumac berry, cactus,
spurge, dropseed, lip fern, corn,
mountain plants, wild potatoes, mesquite,
stems of yucca, tree-yucca flowers, chokecherries,
pitahaya cactus, honey of the ground-bee,
honey, honey of the bumblebee,
mulberries, angle-pod, salt, berries,
berries of the alligator-bark juniper,
wild cattle, mule deer, antelopes,
white-tailed deer, wild turkeys, doves, quail,
squirrels, robins, slate-colored juncoes,
song sparrows, wood rats, prairie dogs,
rabbits, peccaries, burros, mules, horses,
buffaloes, mountain sheep, and turtles.

Gary Snyder

IN THE DEEP CHANNEL

Setting a trotline after sundown
if we went far enough away in the night
sometimes up out of deep water
would come a secret-headed channel cat,

Eyes that were still eyes in the rush of darkness,
flowing feelers noncommittal and black,
and hidden in the fins those rasping bone daggers,
with one spiking upward on its back.

We would come at daylight and find the line sag,
the fishbelly gleam and the rush on the tether:
to feel the swerve and the deep current
which tugged at the tree roots below the river.

WILLIAM STAFFORD

HOW IT BEGAN

They struggled their legs and blindly loved, those puppies
inside my jacket as I walked through town. They crawled
for warmth and licked each other — their poor mother
dead, and one kind boy to save them. I spread
my arms over their world and hurried along.

At Ellen's place I knocked and waited — the tumult
invading my sleeves, all my jacket alive.
When she came to the door we tumbled — black, white,
grey, hungry — all over the living room floor
together, rolling, whining, happy and blind.

WILLIAM STAFFORD

OF MERE BEING

The palm at the end of the mind,
Beyond the last thought, rises
In the bronze decor,

A gold-feathered bird
Sings in the palm, without human meaning,
Without human feeling, a foreign song.

You know then that it is not the reason
That makes us happy or unhappy.
The bird sings. Its feathers shine.

The palm stands on the edge of space.
The wind moves slowly in the branches.
The bird's fire-fangled feathers dangle down.

WALLACE STEVENS

EATING POETRY

Ink runs from the corners of my mouth.
There is no happiness like mine.
I have been eating poetry.

The librarian does not believe what she sees.
Her eyes are sad
and she walks with her hands in her dress.

The poems are gone.
The light is dim.
The dogs are on the basement stairs and coming up.

Their eyeballs roll,
their blond legs burn like brush.
The poor librarian begins to stamp her feet and weep.

She does not understand.
When I get on my knees and lick her hand,
she screams.

I am a new man.
I snarl at her and bark.
I romp with joy in the bookish dark.

MARK STRAND

DO NOT GO GENTLE INTO THAT GOOD NIGHT

Do not go gentle into that good night,
Old age should burn and rave at close of day;
Rage, rage against the dying of the light.

Though wise men at their end know dark is right,
Because their words had forked no lightning they
Do not go gentle into that good night.

Good men, the last wave by, crying how bright
Their frail deeds might have danced in a green bay,
Rage, rage against the dying of the light.

Wild men who caught and sang the sun in flight,
And learn, too late, they grieved it on its way,
Do not go gentle into that good night.

Grave men, near death, who see with blinding sight
Blind eyes could blaze like meteors and be gay,
Rage, rage against the dying of the light.

And you, my father, there on the sad height,
Curse, bless, me now with your fierce tears, I pray.
Do not go gentle into that good night.
Rage, rage against the dying of the light.

DYLAN THOMAS

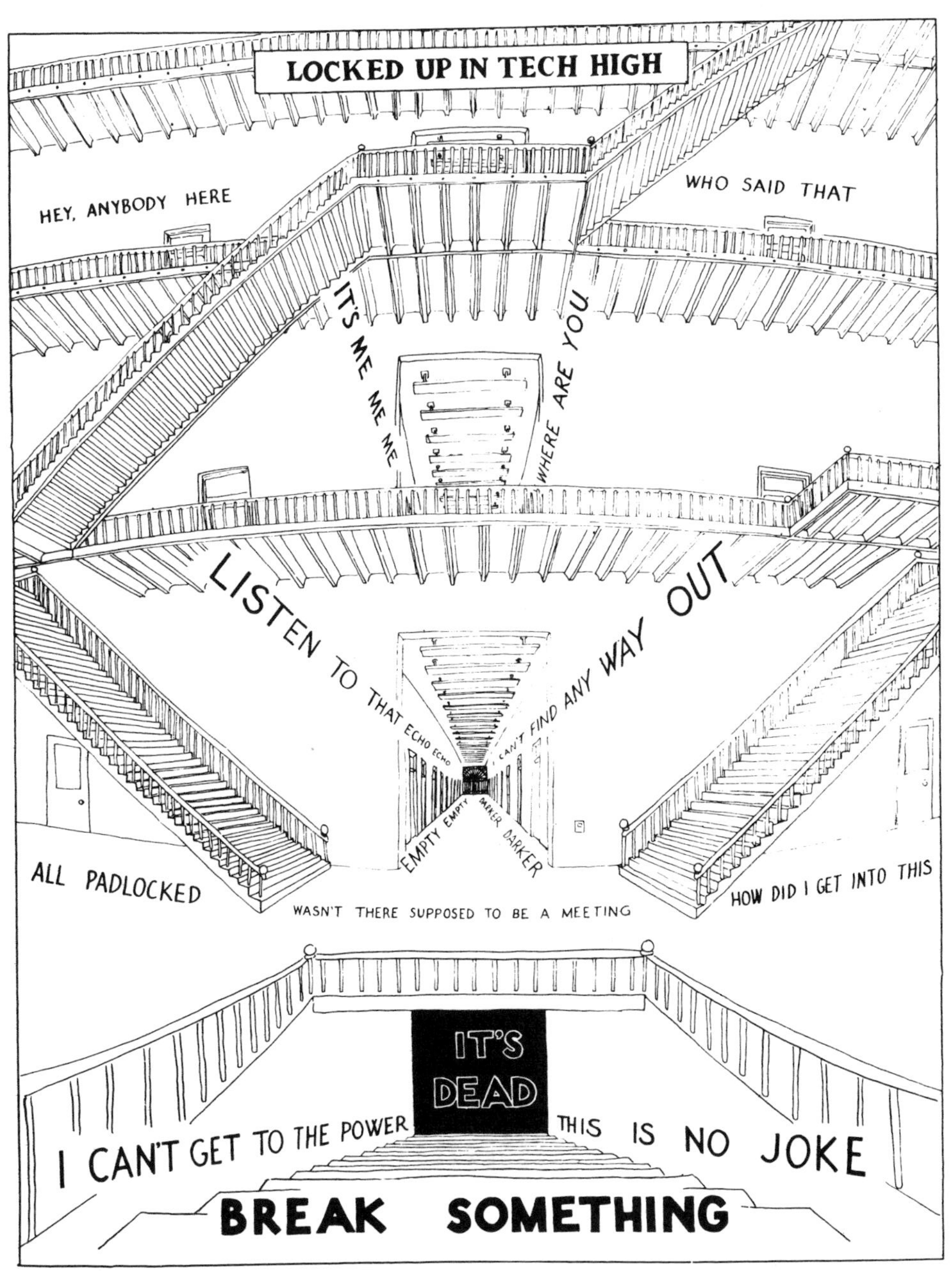

LEONARD TRAWICK

BODY OF —

Feet of clay begin below the knee
like wet socks.
Drying, they arch,
dry, they ache.

The hand of chance folds over its thumb.
Feeling for mouths,
it fingers necks.

The stroke of doom always smooths back
the eye it squeezed out.

The face of truth is bald, with a pulse
and possible ears.
Eyelids rolled back, it stares.

The body of my knowledge has no joints,
counts and keeps counting its legs
and feeling itself for wings.

A. TURNER

ON THE LANGUAGE WHICH WRITES THE LECTURER

This lesson will be on language.
Wittgenstein once asserted that
every language has a structure
concerning which nothing can be said in that language.
We will talk only about what can be said in English.

Our language belongs to the Indo-European group,
subgroup, Germanic. The controllable
units of English are nouns, pronouns,
adjectives, participles, gerunds, verbs
(parsable and unparsable) and dangling modifiers
however inexactly, which convey meaning.

Words are symbolic.
All language is symbolic.
This means that language swallows whole
whatever it refers to and becomes itself the fact.
We will talk only about what can be said in English.

Suppose this: whenever you sit beside a certain girl
you feel a random peace, plain as
cows grazing in the same direction on a hillside.
You think of her and the cows graze in you.
When you evict her, they go.
Therefore she grazes in you often.

Suppose you then say, I have fallen in love.
This is a symbolic statement.
English is an alternative to the language of grazing cows.
Your symbolic English statement neither
slaughters the cows nor brings them home.
You must invent another statement for those facts.

English merely comments on the structure
of another language concerning
which nothing can be said.

This lesson has been on language.

JEANNE WALKER

HOW THINGS HAPPEN

In Lincoln, Nebraska the bell rings
and a woman leans across a desk in classroom 243,
tugging at her white banlon sweater
while she lists the governors from Ashton C. Shallenberger on down.
Hearing a truck outside fail, strip and grind uphill,
her voice skids on a name and goes down.
A fly sizzles and lights on the spiral of a notebook
over which a child bends to erase the name.

Two miles down the street, past houses
you would say were all in the same monotone,
a man in a stone ranch-house leans against the sink,
listening to the regular boom of blood in his wrists.
He is stitching a gauze herb-bag for vegetable soup,
peas, tomatoes, beans, the minimum a child needs to live,
when he thinks he hears on the straightaway outside
a truck catch and growl uphill,
making him forget to listen for the boom.

It is time for the bell to ring.
The bell rings and the child
lets the governors fall to the balls of her feet.
Imagine her walking past carnations deadly
as the gills of slain fish. Past birchtrees
thrust into brown lawns like war staves.
She walks until red moths bang on her eyelids.

When she turns the corner of 54th Street
in the driveway beside the coupe
three men from an emergency squad are at work.

Years later, she finds the soup.

JEANNE WALKER

LOVE CALLS US TO THE THINGS OF THIS WORLD

The eyes open to a cry of pulleys,
And spirited from sleep, the astounded soul
Hangs for a moment bodiless and simple
As false dawn.
Outside the open window
The morning air is all awash with angels.

Some are in bed-sheets, some are in blouses,
Some are in smocks: but truly there they are.
Now they are rising together in calm swells
Of halcyon feeling, filling whatever they wear
With the deep joy of their impersonal breathing;
Now they are flying in place, conveying
The terrible speed of their omnipresence, moving
And staying like white water; and now of a sudden
They swoon down into so rapt a quiet
That nobody seems to be there.
The soul shrinks

From all that it is about to remember,
From the punctual rape of every blesséd day,
And cries,
"Oh, let there be nothing on earth but laundry,
Nothing but rosy hands in the rising steam
And clear dances done in the sight of heaven."

Yet, as the sun acknowledges
With a warm look the world's hunks and colors,
The soul descends once more in bitter love
To accept the waking body, saying now
In a changed voice as the man yawns and rises,

"Bring them down from their ruddy gallows;
Let there be clean linen for the backs of thieves;
Let lovers go fresh and sweet to be undone,
And the heaviest nuns walk in a pure floating
Of dark habits,
keeping their difficult balance."

Richard Wilbur

THIS IS JUST TO SAY

I have eaten
the plums
that were in
the icebox

and which
you were probably
saving
for breakfast

Forgive me
they were delicious
so sweet
and so cold

WILLIAM CARLOS WILLIAMS

THE FIVE DREAMS

What are the five dreams of the elders?

Richard, for all his beard, has seen
mist on an autumn pond and hears
water, the color of cognac, rising
and falling in the reeds of the shallows.
He thrusts his fingers through his hair
and each nail glistens with oil.
He knows that water is giving and taking,
and that it will give and take though fists
slam shut, though the high curse
of his name burns on the door plate.

Wayne is backed against a wall of books,
and the fireplace, the *place* of fire,
reddens his forehead. In his nostrils,
two cables of air freeze, and on them
he hangs in the world. He spreads his arms,
one hand the wing of a leather testament;
the other, the one with a dead ring,
seizes a last book of poetry.
The fire eats all shadows but one.
These were two dreams of the elders.

Emily has brushed her hair forever.
Now it is earth, and pours to her feet.
Half moons glint at her fingertips,
and sand drifts from her mouth, her ears,
the corners of her eyes. She is content.
It was prophesied. Her children look in
at the windows, pale as moonlight.
Remember when they gnawed her breasts?
When she is empty, they will press her
in a book, the book of earth.

Mary knows there are dead places in her.
The doctors, well, the doctors are guessing.
Richard's kiss is dead, but we all
shed layers, and when we have been struck
too often, part of us turns to the wall.
She knows, too, that when the last cobs
of snow melt, green incoherence leaps
from eye to eye. And Wayne's ring?
Well, it turned green before it died.
She takes it off. It pings on the parquet.
The ring scar reddens. She feels better.

This is the last dream of the elders.

Each house has a room that's always locked.
This is the room of dreaming. Sometimes
it is a room of water where a huge eye
glares. Sometimes there is a bed
of glacial sheets, slow, slow, and in them
we can see our gill parents. And, praise God,
one night the young of us will lie down together
in a shallow of black hair. And one day
we will return, put down our cases,
pass through the room where the fist
opens, where the earth sifts, where the ring
spins to quiet. Then, we lie down in
the milky sheets, when the door closes
and is a door no longer.

JOHN WOODS

SAINT JUDAS

When I went out to kill myself, I caught
A pack of hoodlums beating up a man.
Running to spare his suffering, I forgot
My name, my number, how my day began,
How soldiers milled around the garden stone
And sang amusing songs; how all that day
Their javelins measured crowds; how I alone
Bargained the proper coins, and slipped away.

Banished from heaven, I found this victim beaten,
Stripped, kneed, and left to cry. Dropping my rope
Aside, I ran, ignored the uniforms:
Then I remembered bread my flesh had eaten,
The kiss that ate my flesh. Flayed without hope,
I held the man for nothing in my arms.

JAMES WRIGHT

THE SECOND COMING

Turning and turning in the widening gyre
The falcon cannot hear the falconer;
Things fall apart; the center cannot hold;
Mere anarchy is loosed upon the world,
The blood-dimmed tide is loosed, and everywhere
The ceremony of innocence is drowned;
The best lack all conviction, while the worst
Are full of passionate intensity.

Surely some revelation is at hand;
Surely the Second Coming is at hand.
The Second Coming! Hardly are those words out
When a vast image out of *Spiritus Mundi*
Troubles my sight: somewhere in sands of the desert
A shape with lion body and the head of a man,
A gaze blank and pitiless as the sun,
Is moving its slow thighs, while all about it

Reel shadows of the indignant desert birds.
The darkness drops again; but now I know
That twenty centuries of stony sleep
Were vexed to nightmare by a rocking cradle,
And what rough beast, its hour come round at last,
Slouches towards Bethlehem to be born?

W. B. YEATS

WHEN HELEN LIVED

We have cried in our despair
That men desert,
For some trivial affair
Or noisy, insolent sport,
Beauty that we have won
From bitterest hours;
Yet we, had we walked within
Those topless towers
Where Helen walked with her boy,
Had given but as the rest
Of the men and women of Troy,
A word and a jest.

W. B. YEATS

LEDA AND THE SWAN

A sudden blow: the great wings beating still
Above the staggering girl, her thighs caressed
By the dark webs, her nape caught in his bill,
He holds her helpless breast upon his breast.

How can those terrified vague fingers push
The feathered glory from her loosening thighs?
And how can body, laid in that white rush
But feel the strange heart beating where it lies?

A shudder in the loins engenders there
The broken wall, the burning roof and tower
And Agamemnon dead.
Being so caught up,
So mastered by the brute blood of the air,
Did she put on his knowledge with his power
Before the indifferent beak could let her drop?

W. B. YEATS

THE POEM AGAINST THE HORIZON

In a dim room above the freightyards, next to an old brass bed, an angel is taking off his wings. He winces a little as he eases the straps that run down into his chest: the beat of the wings is the beat of the heart.

Out of harness, the heart rolls over now. Panting like a wrestler. Such love, such soaring! Spokane and back. So good to come down, home to this room with the stained lace curtains and the sound of switch engines. So good to remove the wings, the love, the yoke the blood must wear as it paces, oxlike, the circle of its day . . .

He sleeps on his side in the overalls he was too tired to take off. Outside the window, rain runs and drips from the eaves. Overhead, the wind and the black sky belong to someone else.

DAVID YOUNG